Discovering
GERMAN
with

HARRAP

PLANNED AND PRODUCED BY
BOOKMAKER

EDITORIAL DIRECTION
Marie Garagnoux • Patrick Michel-Dansac
WITH
Françoise Avril

COMPILED BY
Bookmaker

TRANSLATION
Dominique Bluher • Maggie Doyle

COLOURS BY
Jean-Pierre Sachse

LETTERING BY
Emile Morteyrol

LAYOUT
Design:
Claudine Roy
Produced by:
Michèle Andrault • Monique Michel-Dansac

OTHERS CONTRIBUTORS
Sylvie Decaux • Elida Mannevy • Tony Page •
Béatrice Leroy • Christine Ehm • Régine Ferrandis •
Mathilde Kemula • Andrea Reule • Catherine Chevalot

PRODUCTION
Véronique Celton

TYPESETTING AND COLOUR SEPARATION
Charente Photogravure

First published by
HARRAP BOOKS Ltd,
43-45 Annandale Street, Edinburgh EH7 4AZ

ISBN 0 245-60394-8

Note to the reader

Mickey, Donald and all their pals are about to help you discover the German language.

You can follow their adventures in the cartoon strips found throughout this book which will introduce you to spoken German. On each page, one of the cartoons has been enlarged and changed (you can have fun spotting the differences); the key words to remember are grouped around the big picture.

Before setting off in your friends' footsteps, read the instructions on page 5 carefully. The guide on page 4 is intended in particular for your parents and teachers.

Foreword

*D*iscovering German with Walt Disney is a vocabulary book for 8 to 13-year-olds, whether beginners or more advanced learners. It includes 1000 words from all grammatical categories (nouns, verbs, adjectives, adverbs, etc.) which have been selected by a team of language teaching specialists. The words, and the sentences in which they appear, correspond to the recommended contents of school curricula. The selection also takes into account the interests and everyday life of children in the 8 to 13 age group.

Each page of the book has been designed to further the joint goals of teaching a basic vocabulary and introducing common expressions: there is a large drawing illustrating the words to be learnt, and a comic strip showing idiomatic phrases in the speech bubbles.

This work is a practical tool which offers the young reader a set of useful guidelines:

• Organisation by areas of meaning puts each new word into a specific context, at once linguistic and visual, revealing its meaning in relation to associated words.

• In the vocabulary pages, the reader discovers original illustrations from the Walt Disney Studios including his or her favourite characters. The authors paid special attention to the quality of the artwork, legibility and careful selection of information.

• Essential basic information such as conjugations, numbers, days and months, etc., are given in separate appendices.

• Two bilingual indexes at the back of the book make up a complete dictionary of its words, and pronunciation is given using international phonetic transcription.

The Walt Disney characters bring their own humour and appeal to this book, which is intended to be, above all, a way to learn German vocabulary and have fun at the same time.

How to use this book

This vocabulary book includes 1000 words, broken down into 10 chapters, each with its own special theme. To learn words about a specific subject, just turn to the relevant chapter about that theme. The chapters go from pages 7 to 93:

The subjects in each chapter are listed on the first page of the chapter. For example, this is the list of subjects on page 7, which is the first page of the chapter on "the house": the garden, the house, in the house, the sitting room, the bedroom, in bed, the kitchen, the bathroom.

These subjects are illlustrated by a large picture surrounded by German words and sentences and their translations.

Under the illustration, a comic strip presents dialogues: the German text comes in the speech bubbles, the translation below.

All the vocabulary words are given in alphabetical order in the two indexes (on pages 101 to 111), along with their translation. If you need the exact translation of a word, simply use the indexes as if you were looking the words up in a dictionary.

You will also find the conjugation tables, the lists of numbers, days and months, as well as phonetics symbols on pages 95 to 99.

das Haus • the house

der Garten • the garden

Er pflanzt einen Baum.
He is planting a tree.

der Rechen
rake

die Gießkanne
watering can

die Hecke
hedge

die Schaufel
shovel

der Rasen
lawn

der Rasenmäher
lawn mower

der Gartenweg
path

Tick gießt die Blumen.
Huey is watering the flowers.

Es ist Frühling, sie sind im Garten.
It is springtime; they are in the garden.

– 'Bye Donald! See you soon!
– 'Bye Daisy!

– Donald

– She loves me… She loves me not…
She loves me…
– She loves me not!

das Haus • the house

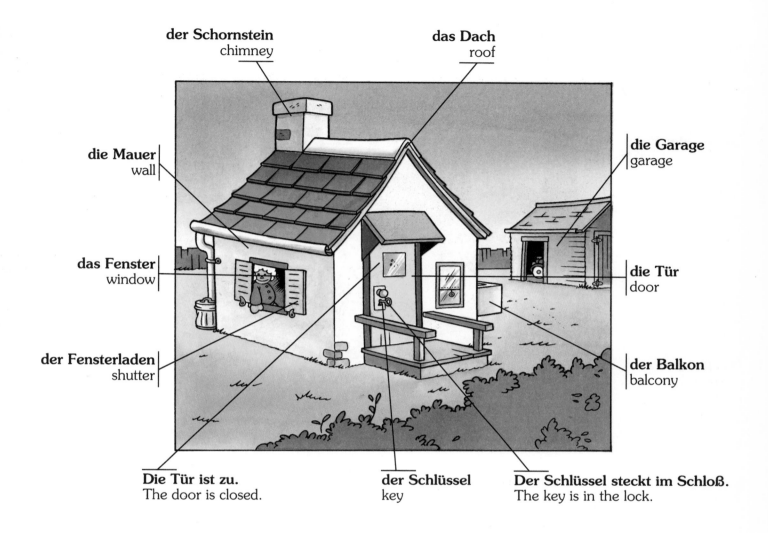

der Schornstein chimney

das Dach roof

die Garage garage

die Mauer wall

das Fenster window

die Tür door

der Fensterladen shutter

der Balkon balcony

Die Tür ist zu. The door is closed.

der Schlüssel key

Der Schlüssel steckt im Schloß. The key is in the lock.

Donald kann nicht in diesem Haus wohnen. Donald cannot live in this house.

– What a lovely house!
– For rent

– You want to rent a house? I can sell you one for only $150.
– Impossible! You can't buy a house for that price!

– You don't believe me? Here's the deed!

– I'll take it!

– Doll's house
– For rent

im Haus • in the house

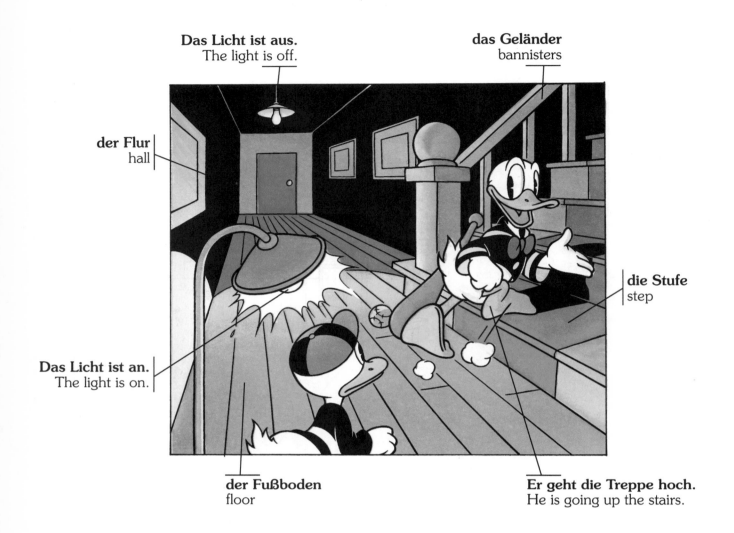

Das Licht ist aus.
The light is off.

das Geländer
bannisters

der Flur
hall

die Stufe
step

Das Licht ist an.
The light is on.

der Fußboden
floor

Er geht die Treppe hoch.
He is going up the stairs.

Der Flur ist schmal und dunkel.
The hall is narrow and dark.

– We're afraid…
– … it's too…
– … dark up there…

– Don't be frightened! Watch me!

das Wohnzimmer · the sitting-room

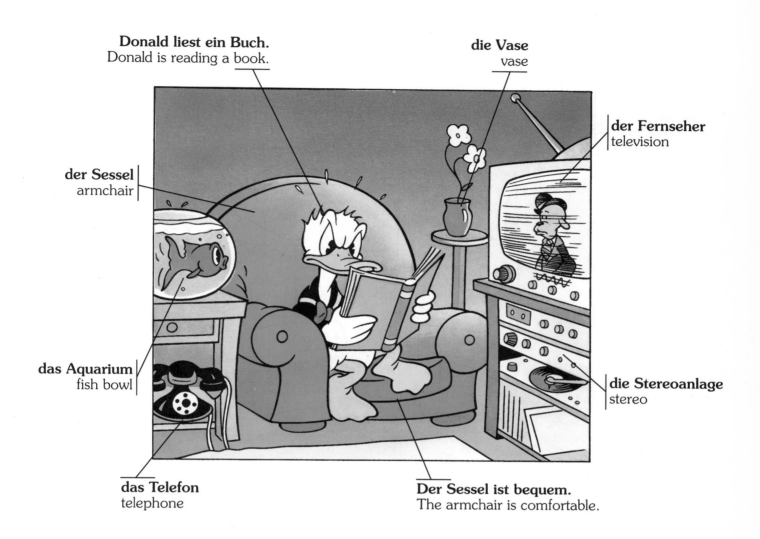

Donald liest ein Buch.
Donald is reading a book.

die Vase
vase

der Fernseher
television

der Sessel
armchair

das Aquarium
fish bowl

das Telefon
telephone

die Stereoanlage
stereo

Der Sessel ist bequem.
The armchair is comfortable.

Donald sitzt.
Donald is sitting down.

Der Goldfisch sieht fern!
The goldfish is watching television!

– That fish is driving me mad!

– Stop staring at me!

das Schlafzimmer • the bedroom

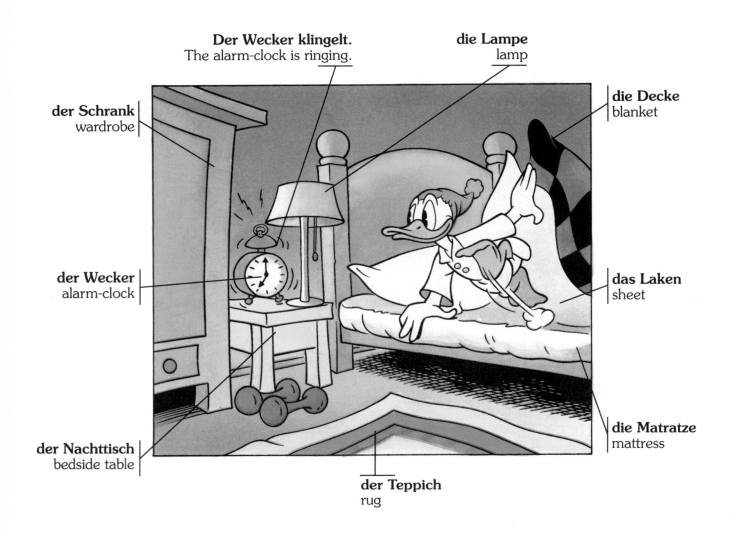

Der Wecker klingelt.
The alarm-clock is ringing.

die Lampe
lamp

der Schrank
wardrobe

die Decke
blanket

der Wecker
alarm-clock

das Laken
sheet

die Matratze
mattress

der Nachttisch
bedside table

der Teppich
rug

Donald steht auf.
Donald is getting up.

Er wird sich bald wieder ins Bett legen.
He will go back to bed soon.

– It's time!

– A little exercice…

– … to wake me up…

– Uh!

im Bett • in bed

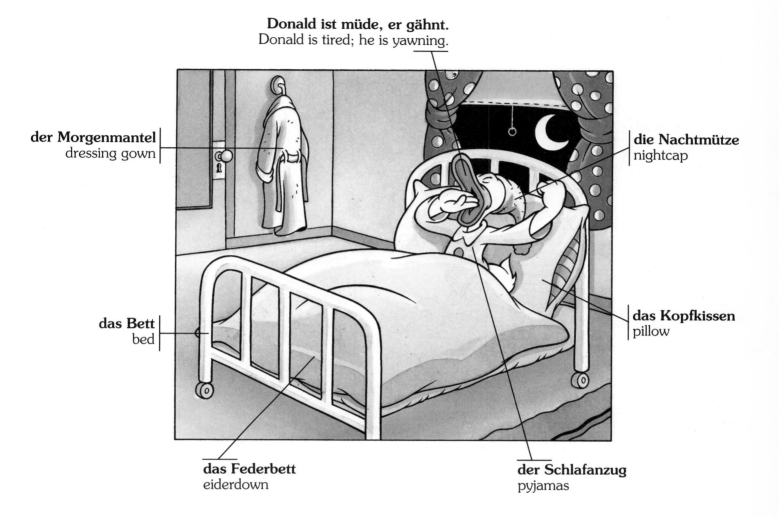

Donald ist müde, er gähnt.
Donald is tired; he is yawning.

der Morgenmantel
dressing gown

die Nachtmütze
nightcap

das Kopfkissen
pillow

das Bett
bed

das Federbett
eiderdown

der Schlafanzug
pyjamas

Es ist spät, es ist Nacht.
It is late; it is nighttime.

Er wird einschlafen.
He is going to sleep.

– Get out of here, you horrible beast!
Let me get some sleep!

die Küche • the kitchen

Donald kocht.
Donald is cooking.

der Kochtopf
saucepan

das Regal
shelf

der Herd
cooker

die Spüle
sink

der Ofen
oven

der Schwamm
sponge

der Mülleimer
dustbin

der Küchenschrank
cupboard

der Hocker
stool

Er hat einen Teller kaputtgemacht.
He broke a plate.

Die Gläser stehen im Regal.
The glasses are kept on the shelf.

Das Geschirr ist nicht gespült.
The dishes are not done.

– It's time... ... to take our...
... medicine, Uncle Donald.

– What a pleasant surprise... no one
is making a face!
– Yum!

– 'Bye!
– 'Bye! This cake will taste better
with some cream...

– Ugh!... Ah!

das Badezimmer • the bathroom

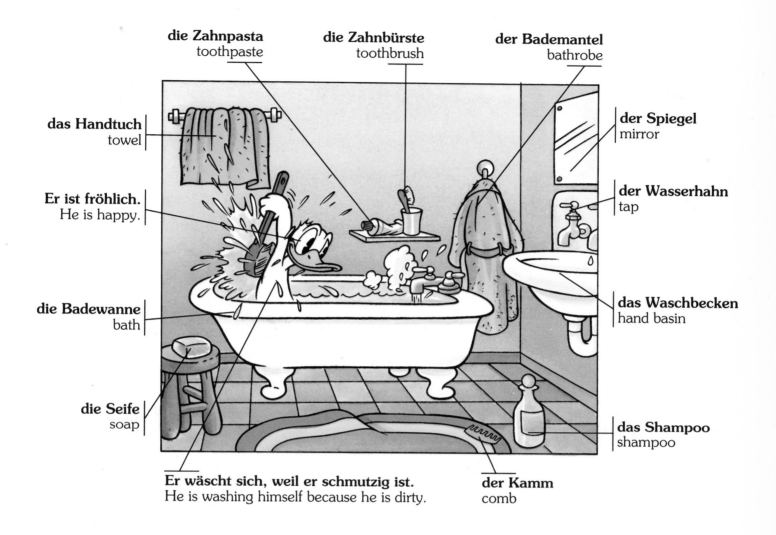

die Zahnpasta
toothpaste

die Zahnbürste
toothbrush

der Bademantel
bathrobe

das Handtuch
towel

der Spiegel
mirror

Er ist fröhlich.
He is happy.

der Wasserhahn
tap

die Badewanne
bath

das Waschbecken
hand basin

die Seife
soap

das Shampoo
shampoo

Er wäscht sich, weil er schmutzig ist.
He is washing himself because he is dirty.

der Kamm
comb

Donald ist reinlich; er badet.
Donald is clean; he is having a bath.

Er putzt sich zweimal täglich die Zähne.
He brushes his teeth twice a day.

– ZZZZ!

– ZZZZ!

die Stadt • the town

die Straße • the street

das Gebäude
building

die Ampel
traffic light

der Bürgersteig
pavement

der Wagen
car

der Polizist
policeman

die Kreuzung
crossroads

Donald fragt den Polizisten nach dem Weg.
Donald is asking the policeman for directions.

Er zeigt ihm den Weg.
He is showing him the way.

Es gibt keinen Stau!
There is no traffic jam!

– No parking

– Car Park

– Post office
– Postmen's bicycles only

der Verkehr • traffic

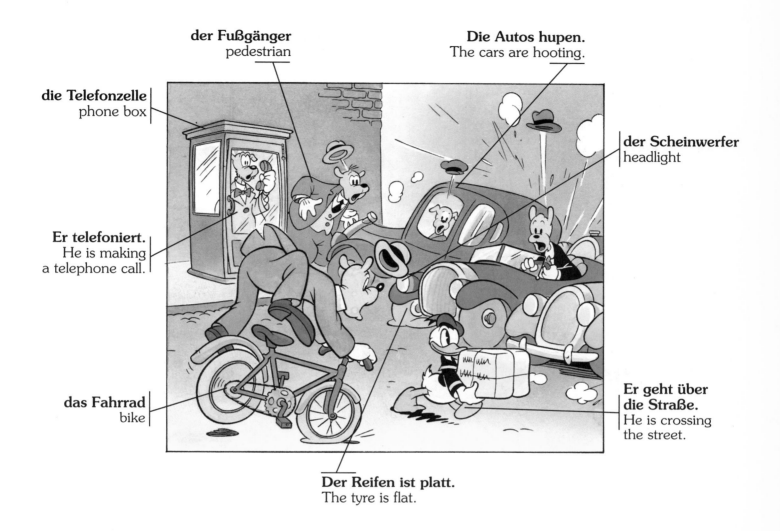

der Fußgänger
pedestrian

Die Autos hupen.
The cars are hooting.

die Telefonzelle
phone box

der Scheinwerfer
headlight

Er telefoniert.
He is making
a telephone call.

das Fahrrad
bike

**Er geht über
die Straße.**
He is crossing
the street.

Der Reifen ist platt.
The tyre is flat.

Donald hat einen Stau verursacht.
Donald has caused a traffic jam.

Man soll glauben, daß in dem Paket Sprengstoff ist.
He gets them to think there is dynamite in the parcel.

– There's only
one way out…

– Danger Dynamite

die Geschäfte • shops

**Es gibt nur eine einzige Bäckerei
in dieser Straße.**
There is only one bakery on this street.

die Fleischerei
butcher's shop

**das
Lebensmittelgeschäft**
grocer's shop

die Bäckerei
bakery

Dieser Laden ist zu.
This shop is closed.

der Bäcker
baker

der Fleischer
butcher

Donald kauft ein.
Donald is shopping.

In dieser Straße gibt es viele Geschäfte.
There are a lot of shops in this street.

Donald geht nicht gern in den Supermarkt.
Donald does not like going to the supermarket.

– This chicken weighs two kilos.
– I'm going to check!
– Stuffed chicken

– Butcher's
– Opening hours

– Don't be offended! I just wanted
to be sure.

– If you didn't shoot it…
– … why is there buckshot…
– … in the stuffing?

das Geld • money

Er verkauft Donald eine Briefmarke.
He is selling Donald a stamp.

der Verkäufer
salesperson

der Geldschein
bank note

die Theke
counter

die Kassiererin
cashier

die Brieftasche
wallet

das Geldstück
coin

Sie zahlt bei der Kassiererin.
She is paying the cashier.

der Geldbeutel
purse

die Kasse
cash register

Donald kauft eine Briefmarke.
Donald is buying a stamp.

Die Milch ist teuer, der Zucker ist billig.
The milk is expensive, the sugar is cheap.

– May I have a two cent stamp?

– Your change!

am Bahnhof • at the station

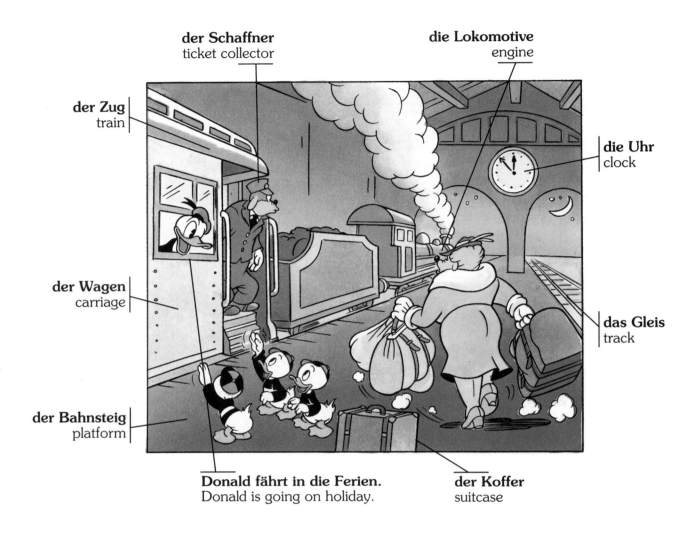

der Schaffner
ticket collector

die Lokomotive
engine

der Zug
train

die Uhr
clock

der Wagen
carriage

das Gleis
track

der Bahnsteig
platform

Donald fährt in die Ferien.
Donald is going on holiday.

der Koffer
suitcase

Die Dame beeilt sich, sie hat sich verspätet.
The woman is in a hurry; she is late.

Ihr Gepäck ist schwer.
Her luggage is heavy.

– See you soon!
– 'Bye…
– Uncle…
– Donald!

– I've forgotten my suitcase!

– Quick! The train is leaving!

die Verkehrsmittel • transport

Er fährt den Bus.
He is driving the bus.

das Schild
road sign

das Taxi
taxi

der Fahrgast
passenger

das Motorrad
motorcycle

der Fahrer
driver

der Bus
bus

der Lastwagen
lorry

der Zebrastreifen
zebra crossing

Sie warten auf den Bus.
They are waiting for the bus.

Das Schild zeigt die Richtungen an.
The road sign gives the directions.

Das kleine Mädchen steht zwischen dem Herrn und der Dame.
The little girl is between the gentleman and the lady.

– Bus stop

– Bus stop

– Bus stop

die Schule • the school

das Klassenzimmer · the classroom

Er ist Klassenbester.
He is top of the class.

Sie wischt die Tafel ab.
She is cleaning the blackboard.

die Tafel
blackboard

die Schülerin
pupil

die Lehrerin
schoolteacher

Sie blättert die Seite um.
She is turning the page.

der Schreibtisch
desk

die Seite
page

der Schüler
pupil

Er schreibt.
He is writing.

Die Schüler sind im Klassenzimmer.
The pupils are in the classroom.

Die Schüler sind fleißig.
The pupils are working hard.

— I'm going to see the headmaster and find out
how Li'l Davy's doing at school…

— Thank you for your help… school is an
excellent influence on Li'l Davy!
— Well…

— I don't know if school has influenced Li'l Davy, but Li'l
Davy has influenced the school!

die Pause • playtime

Der Lehrer beaufsichtigt den Hof.
The teacher is watching the playground.

Er läuft.
He is running.

Die Kinder tanzen Ringelreihen.
The children are dancing in a ring.

Er spielt Murmeln.
He is playing marbles.

Mack hat seine Bücher auf den Boden gelegt.
Morty has put his books on the ground.

Das ist ein Freund von Mack.
He is Morty's friend.

Es ist Pause.
It is playtime.

Die Kinder haben Spaß.
The children are having fun.

Also...du bist der Neue?

– So... You're the new kid?

Stimmt! Noch Fragen?

© 1957
Walt Disney Productions
World Rights Reserved

– That's right! Any more questions?

Was hast du heute in der Schule gelernt, Mack?

Daß der Schein trügt!

– What did you learn at school today, Morty?
– That you can't go by appearances!

das Rechnen · arithmetic

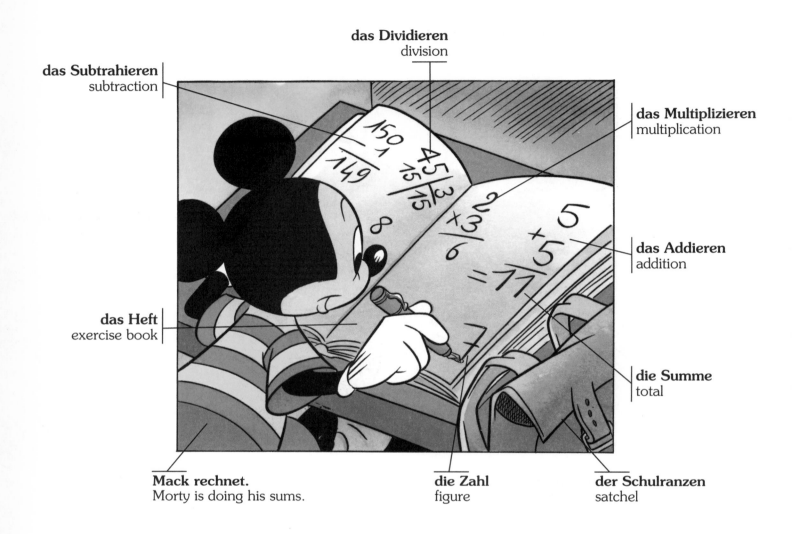

das Dividieren
division

das Subtrahieren
subtraction

das Multiplizieren
multiplication

das Addieren
addition

das Heft
exercise book

die Summe
total

Mack rechnet.
Morty is doing his sums.

die Zahl
figure

der Schulranzen
satchel

Er hat sich verrechnet.
He has made a mistake in one sum.

– Do you want me to help you with your homework?
– X has three dollars pocket money per week.

– Bus fare, pens, sweets, a film a week… X can't do it!
– That's what I thought!

– Thanks for the raise, Mickey!

die Farben • colours

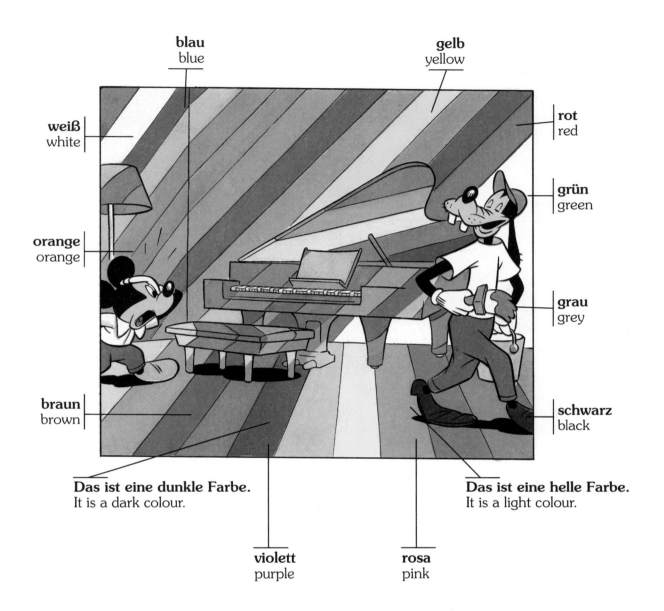

blau
blue

gelb
yellow

weiß
white

rot
red

grün
green

orange
orange

grau
grey

braun
brown

schwarz
black

Das ist eine dunkle Farbe.
It is a dark colour.

Das ist eine helle Farbe.
It is a light colour.

violett
purple

rosa
pink

– Good luck! I hope you'll do a good job!
– What do you mean by that? I paint the best stripes in town!

– Later…
– I don't know why, but I always worry when he does a job for me…

– You said you wanted a good job done… Well, here it is!

die Formen • shapes

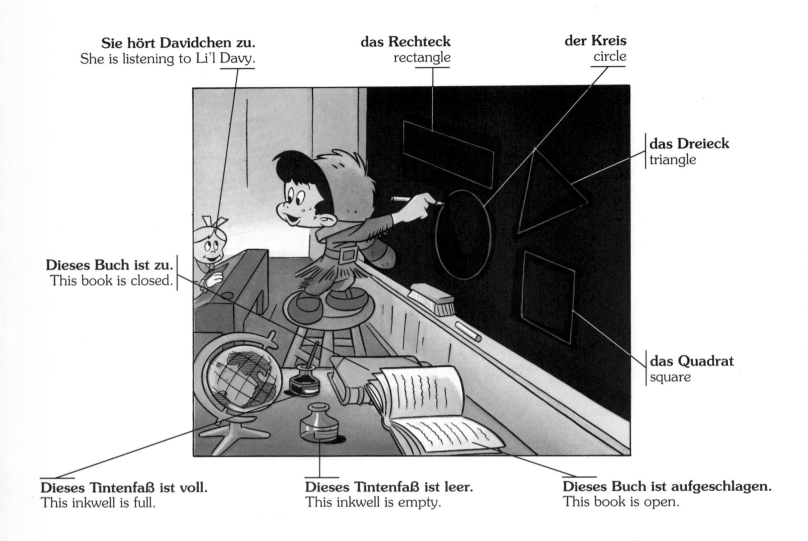

Sie hört Davidchen zu.
She is listening to Li'l Davy.

das Rechteck
rectangle

der Kreis
circle

das Dreieck
triangle

Dieses Buch ist zu.
This book is closed.

das Quadrat
square

Dieses Tintenfaß ist voll.
This inkwell is full.

Dieses Tintenfaß ist leer.
This inkwell is empty.

Dieses Buch ist aufgeschlagen.
This book is open.

Die Erdkugel ist rund.
The globe is round.

– I'm so happy Li'l Davy's going to school!

– At last he's going to learn something…

– And this is a bear track… Has everyone understood?

die Uhrzeit • time

Dieser Zeiger zeigt die Minuten an.
This hand shows the minutes.

Dieser Zeiger zeigt die Stunden an.
This hand shows the hours.

Die Kuckucksuhr geht richtig.
The cuckoo clock is on time.

Goofys Uhr geht nach.
Goofy's watch is slow.

die Armbanduhr
watch

der Wecker
alarm clock

Der Wecker geht vor.
The alarm clock is fast.

Dieser Zeiger zeigt die Sekunden an.
This hand shows the seconds.

Micky zieht den Wecker auf. Er wird morgen früh um 8 Uhr klingeln.
Mickey is winding the alarm clock; it will go off tomorrow morning at eight o'clock.

– Sale
– What a lovely cuckoo clock! I'm so happy I bought it!
– Good luck!

– Now, what time is it?

– It's two o'clock! My cuckoo clock is ringing!

die Leute • people

die Familie • the family

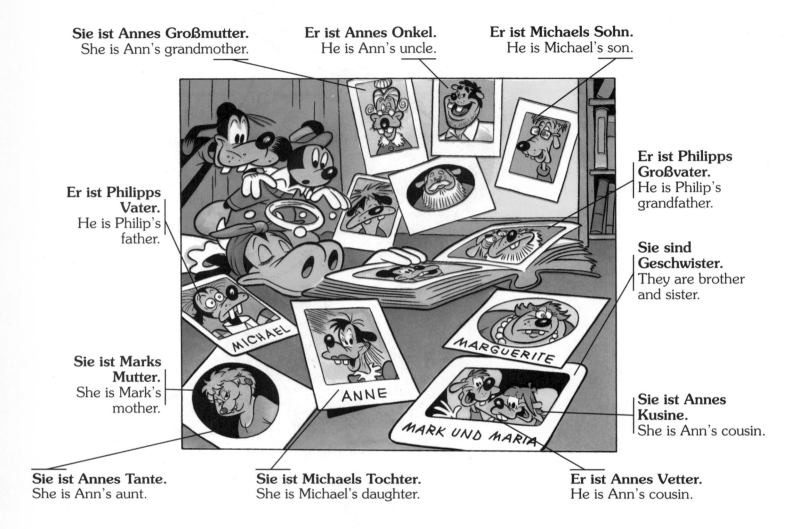

Sie ist Annes Großmutter.
She is Ann's grandmother.

Er ist Annes Onkel.
He is Ann's uncle.

Er ist Michaels Sohn.
He is Michael's son.

Er ist Philipps Vater.
He is Philip's father.

Er ist Philipps Großvater.
He is Philip's grandfather.

Sie sind Geschwister.
They are brother and sister.

Sie ist Marks Mutter.
She is Mark's mother.

Sie ist Annes Kusine.
She is Ann's cousin.

Sie ist Annes Tante.
She is Ann's aunt.

Sie ist Michaels Tochter.
She is Michael's daughter.

Er ist Annes Vetter.
He is Ann's cousin.

Michael ist Margaretes Mann.
Michael is Margaret's husband.

Margarete ist Michaels Frau.
Margaret is Michael's wife.

– See that? She cleans up really well!
– What a mess!

– Crash!

– I never thought you could be afraid of my family…

die Personen • people

die Frau
woman

Er ist glücklich.
He is happy.

Sie ist jung.
She is young.

der Mann
man

das Mädchen
girl

das Baby
baby

Davidchen ist ein Junge.
Li'l Davy is a boy.

Die Mutti hält ihr Baby in den Armen.
The mother is holding her baby in her arms.

Sie hat zwei Kinder.
She has two children.

– You think you can do it?
– Of course! Come and get him in half an hour.

– I'm warning you…
– Now… Now…

– But… But…
– I hate getting my hair cut!

das Aussehen • appearance

Er ist alt.
He is old.

Er ist dick.
He is fat.

Er ist häßlich.
He is ugly.

Er ist groß.
He is tall.

Er ist dünn.
He is thin.

Er ist stark.
He is strong.

Er ist klein.
He is small.

Goofy ist größer als Micky.
Goofy is taller than Mickey.

Micky ist kleiner als Goofy.
Mickey is smaller than Goofy.

Hans ist dicker als Goofy.
John is fatter than Goofy.

– Mickey, do you need an orange squeezer?
– Oh yes, thanks!

– An orange squeezer would be very useful.

– That's really nice of you, Mickey! My cousin was out of work!

das Haar • hair

Er hat kurze Haare.
He has short hair.

der Pferdeschwanz
ponytail

der Pony
fringe

der Schnurrbart
moustache

Sie ist blond.
She is blonde.

Er ist braunhaarig.
He is dark.

der Zopf
plait

der Bart
beard

die Haarspange
slide

Er hat einen Bart und glattes Haar.
He has a beard and straight hair.

Das Mädchen ist rothaarig.
The little girl is red-haired.

Sie hat lange Haare.
She has long hair.

– Mickey, could you pick up my
niece's babysitter?
– Yes…

– You don't mind if I bring my records?

– I'm going to get them to pull over; they look suspicious!

die Persönlichkeit · personality

Micky ist überrascht.
Mickey is surprised.

Davidchen ist höflich.
Li'l Davy is polite.

Goofy ist zufrieden.
Goofy is happy.

Sie ist berühmt.
She is famous.

Goofy ist arm.
Goofy is poor.

Fräulein Latour ist reich.
Miss Latour is rich.

Micky ist nett!
Mickey is nice!

– I'm going hunting!
– OK! But don't bring back an Indian chief or a bear like you usually do…

– Go ahead and laugh, but he often can give you a nasty surprise!

– Later
– I hope you don't mind… I invited…
– No! Certainly not!

– I'm really sorry, Miss Latour!
– It's all right, Li'l Davy!
– I should have kept my mouth shut…

die Kleidung (1) • clothes (1)

die Bluse
blouse

Sie trägt ein schönes, langes Kleid.
She is wearing a lovely evening dress.

die Fliege
bow tie

die Jacke
jacket

der Unterrock
petticoat

die Krawatte
tie

Sie ist sehr elegant.
She looks very smart.

die Strumpfhose
tights

das Kleid
dress

Minnie hat sich geschminkt.
Minnie is wearing make-up.

Micky hat einen neuen Anzug.
Mickey has a new suit.

– Are you going to the dance tonight?
– No, unless I find an old-fashioned girl.

– Did Goofy find a girl he liked?

– Yes! He never does things by halves!

die Kleidung (2) • clothes (2)

der Hut
hat

der Kleiderständer
coatstand

die Schirmmütze
cap

der Mantel
coat

der Regenmantel
raincoat

die Hose
trousers

der Rock
skirt

Seine Jackett ist zu weit.
His jacket is too big.

die Jeans
jeans

Mickys Hosen sind zu kurz.
Mickey's trousers are too short.

Minnie wird sich anziehen.
Minnie is going to get dressed.

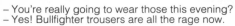

– You're really going to wear those this evening?
– Yes! Bullfighter trousers are all the rage now.

– That evening...
– My first guest... I hope it's Mickey!

– Here we are!

die Kleidung (3) • clothes (3)

der Kleiderschrank
wardrobe

das T-shirt
tee-shirt

der Pullover
pullover

das Hemd
shirt

der Gürtel
belt

die Hausschuhe
slippers

die Schublade
drawer

die Socken
socks

Im Kleiderschrank hängen viele Kleider.
There are a lot of clothes in the wardrobe.

Er hat seine Mütze am Kleiderständer aufgehängt.
He has hung his cap on the peg.

– Thanks to this spray, there'll be no more moths…

– They'll never know what hit them…

– Later…
– I've forgotten my best suit!

die Schuhe • shoes

Sein Stiefel hat ein Loch.
There is a hole in his boot.

Sein Fuß tut ihm weh.
His foot hurts.

der Sportschuh
tennis shoe

der Stiefel
boot

der Schnürsenkel
shoelace

der Halbstiefel
ankle boot

der Absatz
heel

der Pumps
court shoe

Goofys Schuhe sind zu groß.
Goofy's shoes are too big.

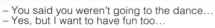

– You said you weren't going to the dance…
– Yes, but I want to have fun too…

– That's strange…
– What's it to you?

– I couldn't stand people stepping on my feet anymore.

der Schmuck • jewellery

der Ring
ring

Dieser Goldring glänzt.
This gold ring glitters.

der Ohrring
earring

der Smaragd
emerald

die Perle
bead

die Halskette
necklace

das Armband
bracelet

Minnies Kette ist kaputt.
Minnie's necklace broke.

die Brosche
brooch

der Rubin
ruby

Die Perlen sind auf den Boden gerollt.
The beads rolled on the floor.

Smaragde und Rubine sind Edelsteine.
Emeralds and rubies are precious stones.

– Mickey! My beads…!
– I'll pick them up for you!

– Gosh! There are a lot of them!

– There… I think I've got them all…

– Everyone else went home long ago!

der menschliche Körper • the human body

die Körperteile (1) • parts of the body (1)

der Kopf
head

Er runzelt die Stirn.
He is frowning.

die Schulter
shoulder

der Hals
neck

der Bauch
stomach

der Hintern
bottom

der Rücken
back

Sie trägt eine Brille.
She is wearing glasses.

Die Dame dreht Donald den Rücken zu.
The lady is turning her back on Donald.

– Hey, you! Can't you see I'm taking a photo?

– Oh, Oscar!

die Körperteile (2) • parts of the body (2)

Er verschränkt die Arme.
His arms are crossed.

Der Masseur steht.
The masseur is standing up.

das Bein
leg

der Arm
arm

der Finger
finger

der Fuß
foot

der Ellenbogen
elbow

Er trägt Sandalen.
He is wearing sandals.

die Hand
hand

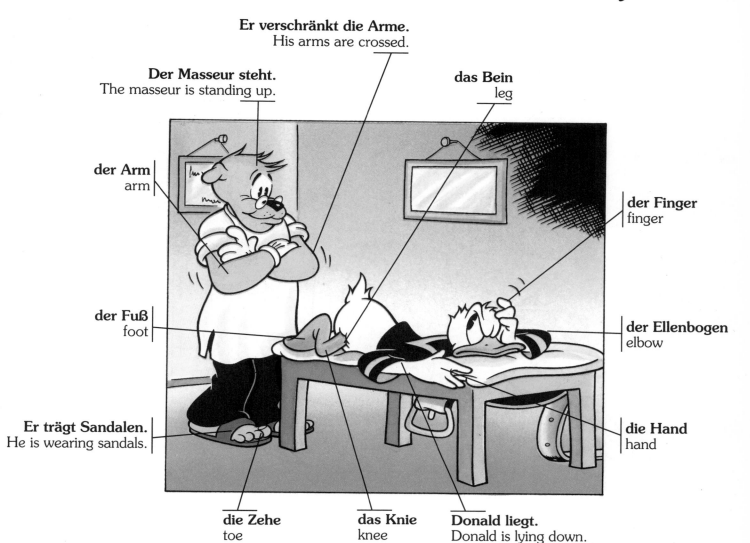

die Zehe
toe

das Knie
knee

Donald liegt.
Donald is lying down.

Der Masseur hat muskulöse Arme.
The masseur's arms are well-muscled.

Donald läßt sich einmal wöchentlich massieren.
Donald has a massage once a week.

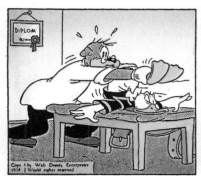

– Diploma

– Crack

– That'll be one dollar, sir!

das Gesicht • the face

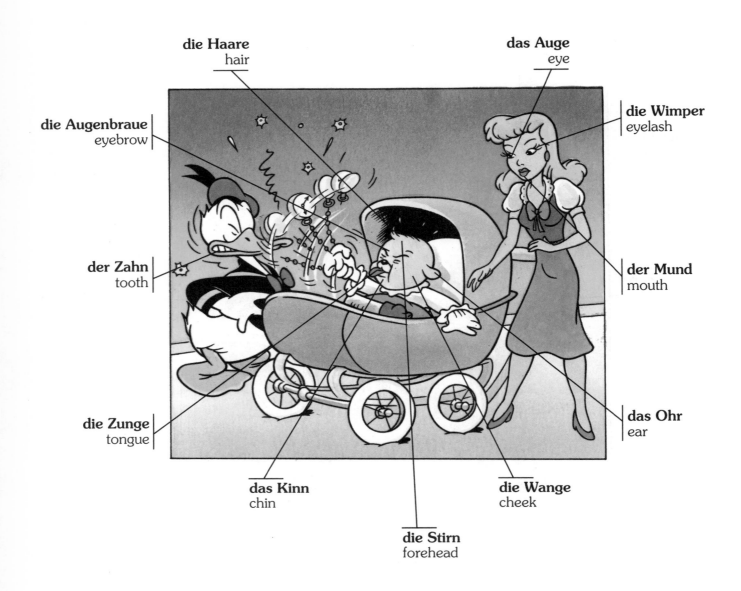

die Haare
hair

das Auge
eye

die Augenbraue
eyebrow

die Wimper
eyelash

der Zahn
tooth

der Mund
mouth

die Zunge
tongue

das Ohr
ear

das Kinn
chin

die Wange
cheek

die Stirn
forehead

Das Baby streckt die Zunge raus.
The baby is sticking out his tongue.

– Oh! Aren't you cute!
Cootchy, cootchy coo!

– Shh!
– Boohoo!

– Look! The watch is
going tick-tock!

die Gesundheit • health

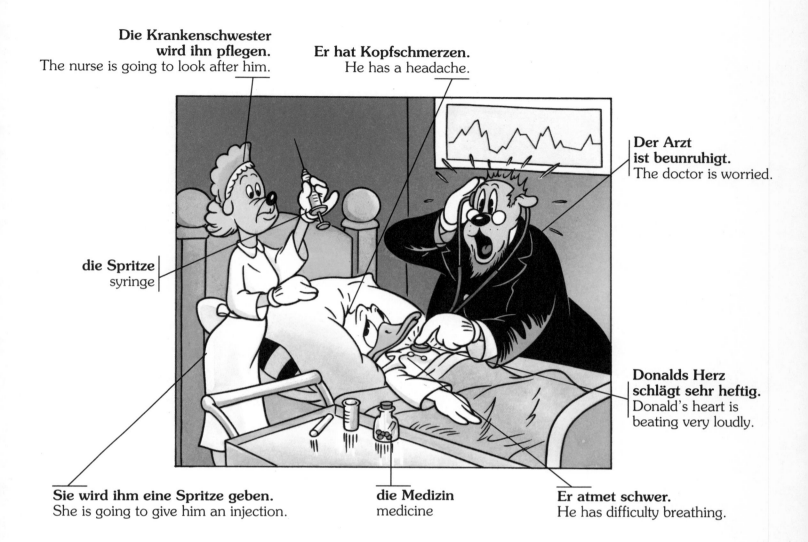

Die Krankenschwester wird ihn pflegen.
The nurse is going to look after him.

Er hat Kopfschmerzen.
He has a headache.

Der Arzt ist beunruhigt.
The doctor is worried.

die Spritze
syringe

Sie wird ihm eine Spritze geben.
She is going to give him an injection.

die Medizin
medicine

Donalds Herz schlägt sehr heftig.
Donald's heart is beating very loudly.

Er atmet schwer.
He has difficulty breathing.

Man hat ihn mit dem Krankenwagen ins Krankenhaus gebracht.
He was brought to the hospital by ambulance.

Donald wird vielleicht sterben.
Perhaps Donald will die.

– I'll pretend to be sick…

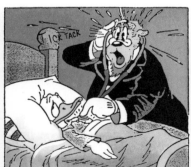
– Tick tock

– Ha ha! That fooled him!

– Ambulance

die Nahrung • food

das Gemüse • vegetables

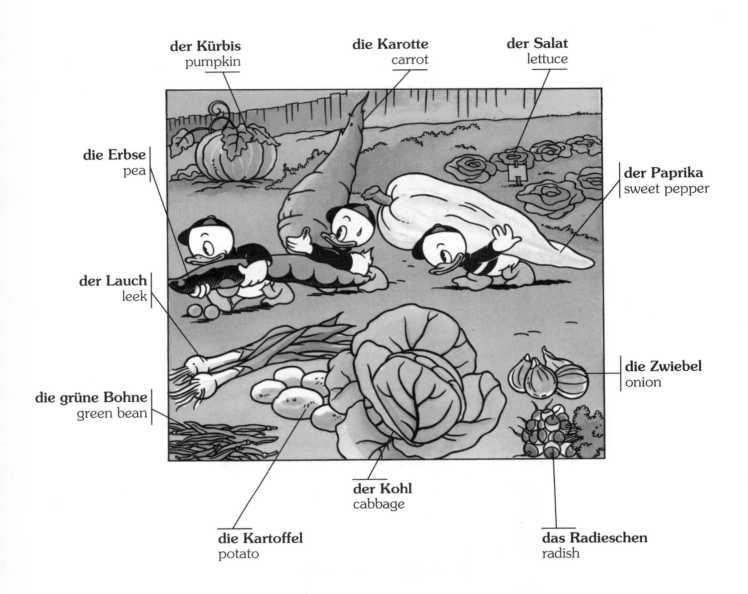

der Kürbis
pumpkin

die Karotte
carrot

der Salat
lettuce

die Erbse
pea

der Paprika
sweet pepper

der Lauch
leek

die Zwiebel
onion

die grüne Bohne
green bean

der Kohl
cabbage

die Kartoffel
potato

das Radieschen
radish

– We bought some… … magic fertilizer.
– Magic fertilizer
– You know, it's rain and work that make plants grow…

– It's raining! I bet everything will have grown by tomorrow!

– Morning
– I can't wait to see…

– There! I told you everything would have…
– … grown!

das Obst · fruit

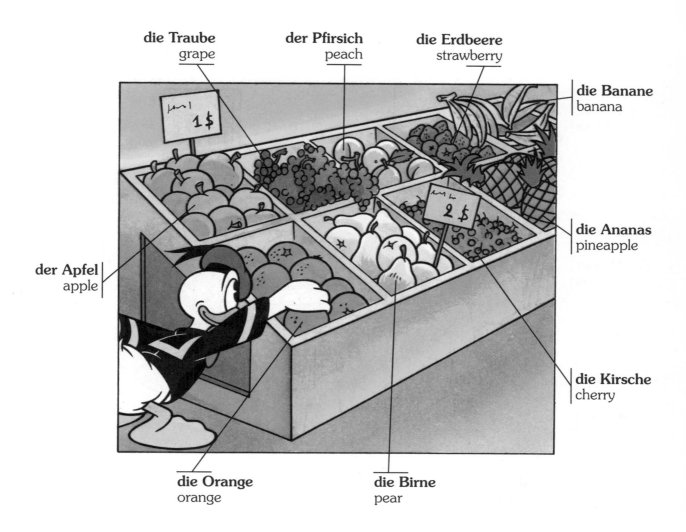

die Traube
grape

der Pfirsich
peach

die Erdbeere
strawberry

die Banane
banana

der Apfel
apple

die Ananas
pineapple

die Kirsche
cherry

die Orange
orange

die Birne
pear

Das Obst ist reif.
The fruit is ripe.

Der Pfirsich ist eine Frucht.
A peach is a piece of fruit.

– Have you seen the lovely fruit?

– Do you want any more?

der Tisch • the table

das Salz
salt

der Pfeffer
pepper

der Stuhl
chair

das Messer
knife

die Serviette
napkin

der Löffel
spoon

die Gabel
fork

das Glas
glass

der Teller
plate

Donald hält eine Platte.
Donald is holding a dish.

Franz Gans ist immer hungrig und durstig.
Gus Goose is always hungry and thirsty.

– There! I hope that's enough!

– Oh dear! He's so greedy!
I hope he leaves me something
to eat…

– What? There's nothing left but the…

– … bones?

das Frühstück • breakfast

Donald trinkt Kaffee.
Donald is drinking coffee.

die Tasse
cup

die Milch
milk

das Müsli
cereal

das Ei
egg

die Marmelade
jam

die Butter
butter

die Teekanne
teapot

die Kaffeekanne
coffee-pot

der Honig
honey

der Zucker
sugar

das Brot
bread

Er hat Tee gekocht.
He has got tea ready.

Die Neffen sind noch nicht aufgestanden.
The nephews are not up yet.

– This coffee has no sugar in it…

– This sugar dispenser really isn't very practical…

– I've a solution!

das Mittagessen • lunch

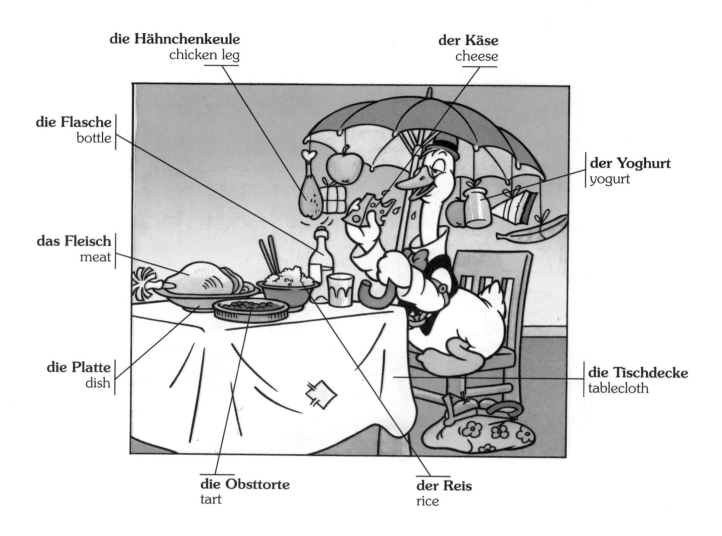

die Hähnchenkeule
chicken leg

der Käse
cheese

die Flasche
bottle

der Yoghurt
yogurt

das Fleisch
meat

die Platte
dish

die Tischdecke
tablecloth

die Obsttorte
tart

der Reis
rice

Franz Gans ißt viel.
Gus Goose eats a lot.

Der Käse ist köstlich.
The cheese is delicious.

– You see? There's nothing to eat!

– It worked! He's going back to his house!

– Plop!

das Abendessen • dinner

Franz Gans hat den Kühlschrank ausgeräumt!
Gus Goose has emptied the fridge!

Die Suppe ist kochend heiß.
The soup is boiling hot.

Donald ist zornig.
Donald is angry.

das Wasser
water

die Pfanne
frying pan

die Suppenschüssel
soup tureen

die Suppenkelle
ladle

die Suppe
soup

der Fisch
fish

Franz Gans ist kein echter Schlafwandler!
Gus Goose is not a real sleepwalker!

Er mag Fisch.
He likes fish.

– Where is he going?

– Into the kitchen?

die Natur • nature

der Wald • the forest

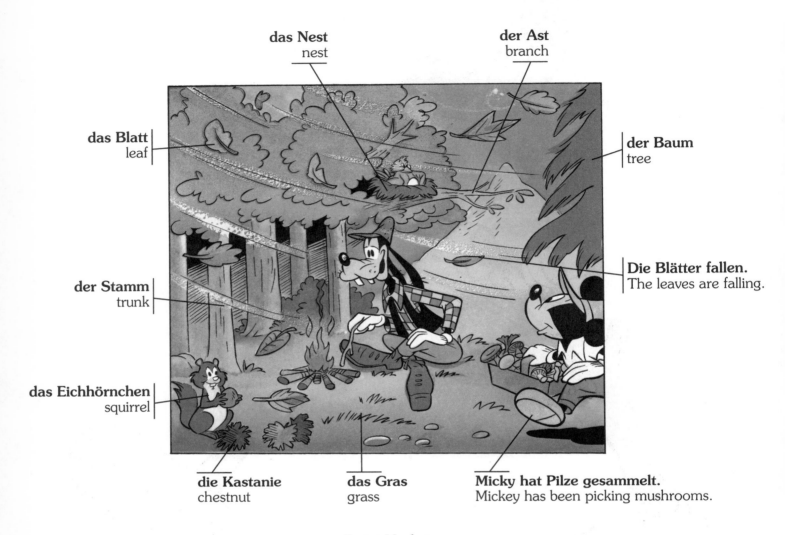

das Nest
nest

der Ast
branch

das Blatt
leaf

der Baum
tree

der Stamm
trunk

Die Blätter fallen.
The leaves are falling.

das Eichhörnchen
squirrel

die Kastanie
chestnut

das Gras
grass

Micky hat Pilze gesammelt.
Mickey has been picking mushrooms.

Es ist Herbst.
It is autumn.

Sie sind auf einer Lichtung.
They are in a clearing.

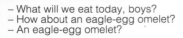

– What will we eat today, boys?
– How about an eagle-egg omelet?
– An eagle-egg omelet?

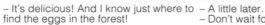

– It's delicious! And I know just where to
find the eggs in the forest!

– A little later…
– Don't wait for me! I may be a little late!

das Gebirge • the mountains

die Gemse
chamois

der Berg
mountain

der Gipfel
peak

der Adler
eagle

das Reh
deer

die Hütte
chalet

Goofy ist hinter Micky.
Goofy is behind Mickey.

der Weg
track

der Gebirgsbach
mountain stream

Micky ist vor Goofy.
Mickey is in front of Goofy.

Das Tal ist unten.
The valley is below.

Der Gipfel ist oben.
The peak is above.

– It's fun collecting birds' eggs for the museum...
– Let's keep in touch on the walkie-talkie!

– Later...
– Bzzz Bzzz
– I wonder what Goofy wants...

– Have you found anything?
– No, I'm the one who's been found!

das Land • the countryside

der Vogel
bird

Der Vogel fliegt.
The bird is flying.

die Kuh
cow

das Kalb
calf

das Schwein
pig

der Zaun
fence

die Wiese
meadow

das Kaninchen
rabbit

der Bach
brook

die Ziege
goat

Die Sonne geht auf: es ist sehr früh.
The sun is rising: it is very early.

Welch schöne Landschaft!
What a beautiful landscape!

– It's too dangerous to drive in this fog! I'll pull over and wait.

– Morning...
– I fell asleep! At last the fog's lifted...

– One thing is certain, it was very foggy!

die Blumen • flowers

die Rose
rose

die Nelke
carnation

der Strauß
bouquet

die Tulpe
tulip

die Biene
bee

der Stengel
stem

Das riecht gut!
What a lovely smell!

Diese Blume ist verblüht.
This flower has wilted.

die Blütenblätter
petals

die Margerite
daisy

Es gibt nur Blumen, es gibt keine Grünpflanzen.
There are only flowers here; there are no green plants.

– Oh! I'm sorry!
– Florist

– Minnie, just let me explain!

der Fluß • the river

die Angel fishing rod

der Fisch fish

das Ufer bank

der Angler fisherman

die Tanne fir tree

der Kieselstein pebble

die Brücke bridge

Er hat einen schönen Fisch geangelt.
He caught a fine fish.

das Kanu canoe

Der Fluß ist tief.
The river is deep.

Das Wasser fließt unter der Brücke.
The water is flowing under the bridge.

– It's a real canoe… I built it just like the Indians do!
– It doesn't look very sturdy…

– We're sinking!
– No we aren't! In a minute, we'll be in the middle of the river!

– Come back, Goofy! Come back!

das Meer • the sea

der Anker
anchor

das Schiff
ship

der Leuchtturm
lighthouse

Er fährt Wasserschi.
He is water-skiing.

die Mole
jetty

das Boot
boat

Er schwimmt.
He is swimming.

Es ist ein Schiff im Hafen.
There is a ship in the harbour.

Der Wind bläst.
The wind is blowing.

– Get the sail down! There's too much wind!
– I'm trying!

– Mickey!
– I can't do it!

– Police
– I don't suppose you'd be interested in an explanation…

der Himmel • the sky

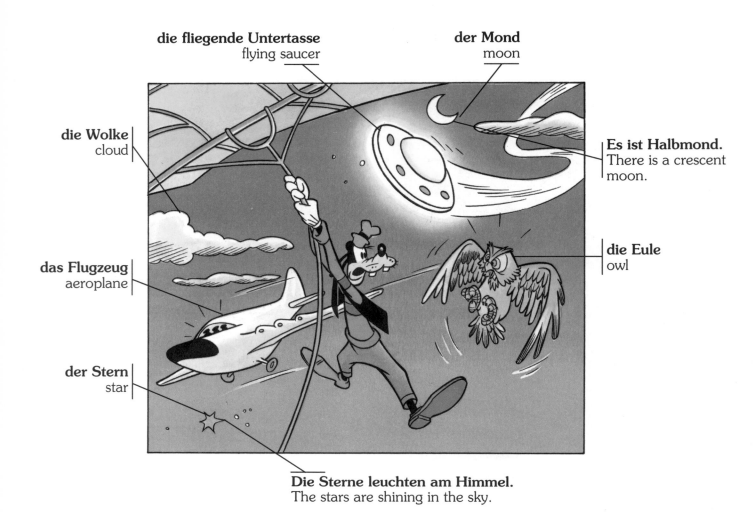

die fliegende Untertasse
flying saucer

der Mond
moon

die Wolke
cloud

Es ist Halbmond.
There is a crescent moon.

das Flugzeug
aeroplane

die Eule
owl

der Stern
star

Die Sterne leuchten am Himmel.
The stars are shining in the sky.

Die fliegende Untertasse fliegt durch die Luft.
The flying saucer is crossing the sky.

Die Nacht ist unruhig.
It is a hectic night.

– I've got an idea! I'm going to make my kite just like a seagull!
– I see...

– There we are! I'm flying away like a... Aaah!

– OK, now explain how I get back down!

der Sturm • the storm

Goofy stellt sich im Haus unter.
Goofy is sheltering inside the house.

der Blitz
lightning

der Regenschirm
umbrella

der Regenmantel
raincoat

der Regen
rain

die Pfütze
puddle

Mickys Schuhe sind naß.
Mickey's shoes are wet.

Es ist windig!
It is windy!

Man hört den Donner.
Thunder can be heard.

– I'm going to hang up my barometer and see what the weather will be… Oops!

– It's stuck!
– Fine
– Rain

– I think I did something silly…

der Bauernhof • the farm

die Katze
cat

der Hahn
cock

Die Katze ist auf dem Dach.
The cat is on the roof.

Das Huhn ist im Hühnerstall.
The hen is in the henhouse.

der Bauer
farmer

das Pferd
horse

das Huhn
hen

der Hund
dog

die Ente
duck

die Hundehütte
kennel

Die Ente schwimmt auf dem Teich.
The duck is swimming in the pond.

das Schwein
pig

**Er ist ein zuverlässiger Hund;
er bewacht das Haus.**
The dog is faithful; he is guarding the house.

Wie viele Tiere gibt es?
How many animals are there?

Der Bauer reitet.
The farmer is riding his horse.

– I've decided to put a weathercock on my roof!
– That's a good idea!

– A few days later…
– I'm going to see Goofy… His
weathercock must be ready by now…

– I think I must have got the instructions wrong…

68

die wilden Tiere • wild animals

die Giraffe
giraffe

das Nilpferd
hippopotamus

der Affe
monkey

Das Zebra läuft schnell.
The zebra is running quickly.

der Elefant
elephant

der Löwe
lion

Micky hat Angst vor wilden Tieren.
Mickey is afraid of wild animals.

die Schlange
snake

das Krokodil
crocodile

Vorsicht! Der Löwe sieht böse aus.
Watch out! The lion looks cross.

Die Giraffe hat einen langen Hals.
The giraffe has a long neck.

– But, Minnie... I didn't want my sitting-room papered.
– Come and see how amazing these new wallpapers are!

– See! It looks like a real garden! Do you like it?
– Yes... I almost thought...

– Wait and see what I have chosen for your sitting-room!...

– Later

Freizeit • leisure

der Flughafen • the airport

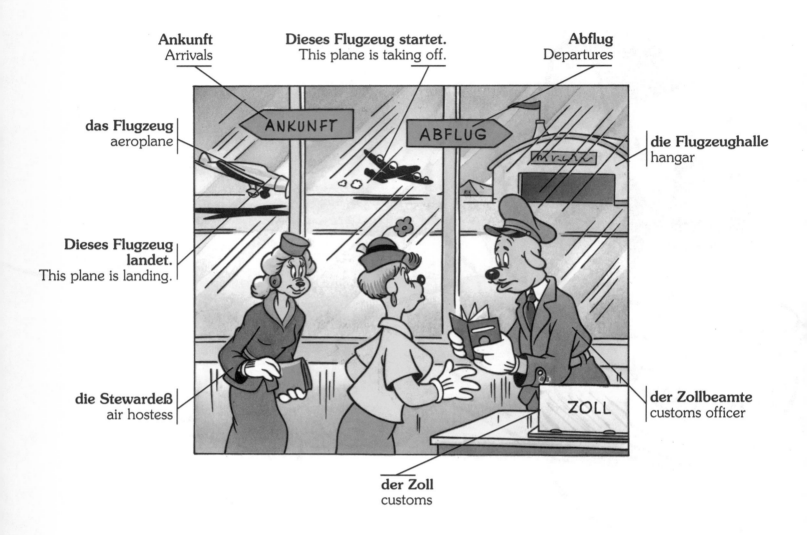

Ankunft
Arrivals

Dieses Flugzeug startet.
This plane is taking off.

Abflug
Departures

das Flugzeug
aeroplane

die Flugzeughalle
hangar

Dieses Flugzeug landet.
This plane is landing.

die Stewardeß
air hostess

der Zollbeamte
customs officer

der Zoll
customs

Eine Frau zeigt dem Zollbeamten ihren Paß.
A woman is showing her passport to the customs officer.

– You can land the plane today...
– But... But...

– That's it! Go easy now!

– Bravo! I couldn't have done better!
– Help!

der Strand • the beach

die Palme
palm tree

Die Sonne scheint.
The sun is shining.

Er baut eine Sandburg.
He is building a sand castle.

der Sonnenschirm
beach umbrella

die Sonnenbrille
sunglasses

der Badeanzug
bathing suit

der Schwimmring
rubber ring

die Muscheln
shells

der Sand
sand

Sie ist braun.
She is sun-tanned.

Sie sind im Urlaub.
They are on holiday.

Es ist schönes Wetter, es ist Sommer.
The weather is fine; it is summer.

– There're a lot of people here!...

– Where can I sit?

der Campingplatz • camping

das Wohnmobil
camping car

der Wohnwagen
caravan

der Rauch
smoke

das Zelt
tent

der Schlafsack
sleeping bag

das Feuer
fire

der Rucksack
rucksack

die Gitarre
guitar

Er grillt Fleisch.
He is grilling the meat.

das Holz
wood

Micky wärmt sich am Feuer.
Mickey is warming himself beside the fire.

Micky zeltet furchtbar gern.
Mickey loves camping.

– Well, Goofy, are you glad you slept in the great outdoors?
– Yes…

– Luckily, I had my sleeping bag to keep me warm!
– Yes… It was cold last night…

– Very cold!

Spielsachen und Spiele • toys and games

der Ball
ball

das Mobile
mobile

der Dominostein
domino

der Teddybär
teddy bear

das Damespiel
checkers

das Schachspiel
chess

das Damebrett
draught-board

das Puzzle
puzzle

die Puppe
doll

der Bauklotz
building block

Das Puzzle ist nicht fertig.
The puzzle is not finished.

Das Spielzimmer ist unordentlich.
The playroom is untidy.

Die Puppe heißt Caroline.
The doll's name is Caroline.

– Come on, Morty! It's bedtime!
– I want to keep playing, Mickey!

– You go to bed!
– I was having such fun with you!

– This game of dominos was so boring! I prefer Morty's toys!
– Me too!

der Zoo • the zoo

die Giraffe
giraffe

das Känguruh
kangaroo

der Hirsch
stag

der Pinguin
penguin

der Strauß
ostrich

das Zebra
zebra

Das Känguruh springt.
The kangaroo is jumping.

das Kamel
camel

Der Pinguin fängt einen Fisch.
The penguin is catching a fish.

Der Strauß versteckt sich.
The ostrich is hiding.

– What are you talking about?
My ostrich is a bad influence on
the other animals?

– O.K. I'll go to the zoo and see what's
happening.

das Gemälde • painting

der Bleistift
pencil

das Lineal
ruler

der Radiergummi
rubber

Dieses Bild ist ein Meisterwerk!
This painting is a masterpiece!

Er hat Farbflecken auf seinem Kittel.
There are paint stains on his smock.

die Palette
palette

die Leinwand
canvas

die Farbtube
tube of paint

das Papier
paper

der Pinsel
paint brush

Der Künstler malt gut.
The artist paints well.

Er hat ein Porträt von Donald gemacht.
He has painted Donald's portrait.

– It's really not expensive…
– I've got to eat! I'm a poor starving artist!
– Portraits painted $ 2

die Musik • music

das Klavier
piano

die Trompete
trumpet

der Dirigent
conductor

die Flöte
flute

Er dirigiert das Orchester.
He is conducting the orchestra.

die Bühne
stage

Er spielt Geige.
He is playing the violin.

die Geige
violin

Das Publikum applaudiert.
The audience is clapping.

– I didn't know you were giving a concert here.
– Oh really?
– Stage door

das Konzert • the concert

Er ist ein guter Musiker.
He is a good musician.

der Sänger
singer

die elektrische Gitarre
electric guitar

das Saxophon
saxophone

das Mikro
microphone

das Schlagzeug
drums

der Synthesizer
synthesizer

Er singt falsch.
He is singing out of tune.

Alle tanzen.
Everybody is dancing.

– Music competition

– Later
– A harp?
– Yes! I changed my instrument!

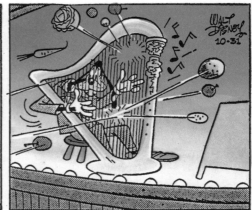

das Kino • the cinema

der Schauspieler
actor

Der Held verteidigt sich.
The hero fights back.

der Projektor
projector

der Held
hero

die Leinwand
screen

der Sessel
seat

der Gang
aisle

Er schreit.
He is screaming.

Die Zuschauer sind gefesselt.
The viewers are enthralled.

Wie spannend!
How exciting!

Der Film ist unheimlich.
The film is scary.

– I just love horror films… I can't see the screen…

– Excuse me, could you take your hat off?

– Arrgh!

der Park • the park

Er rutscht die Rutschbahn runter.
He is sliding down the slide.

der Brunnen
fountain

die Rutschbahn
slide

der Wächter
park attendant

die Bank
bench

die Schaukel
swing

der Kinderwagen
pushchair

– I'm thirsty!

der Sport • sport

der Sportplatz • the stadium

der Champion
champion

Er springt.
He is jumping.

der Sieger
winner

die Medaille
medal

das Podium
podium

die Rennbahn
track

Er hat gewonnen.
He won.

Goofy läuft.
Goofy is running.

– Forget the other athletes. Concentrate on the race: close your eyes and run!
– You can depend on me!

– Goofy!
– Finish

– I think I can open my eyes now…

die Ausrüstung • sportsgear

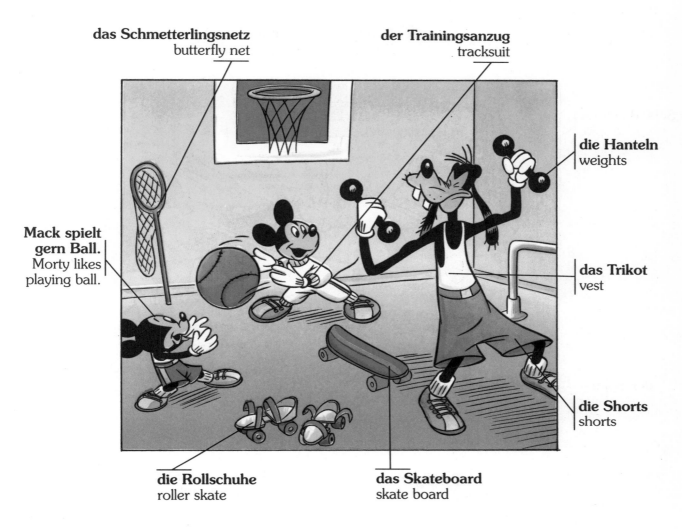

das Schmetterlingsnetz
butterfly net

der Trainingsanzug
tracksuit

die Hanteln
weights

das Trikot
vest

Mack spielt gern Ball.
Morty likes playing ball.

die Shorts
shorts

die Rollschuhe
roller skate

das Skateboard
skate board

Sie sind in der Sporthalle.
They are in the gym.

Minnie macht lieber Gymnastik.
Minnie prefers gymnastics.

– I must get a little exercise.

– It really is strong for a butterfly!

– You've given up chasing butterflies?
– Yes, it's too dangerous!

das Tischtennis • table tennis

Goofy gewinnt gerade das Spiel.
Goofy is winning the match.

der Schiedsrichter
umpire

der Tischtennisball
ball

der Spieler
player

das Netz
net

der Schläger
bat

die Tischtennisplatte
ping pong table

Dieser Ball hat das Spiel entschieden.
It is the match point.

– You play well Goofy, but you wave your arms a lot!
– I'm so excited by the game that I can't keep still.

das Schifahren · skiing

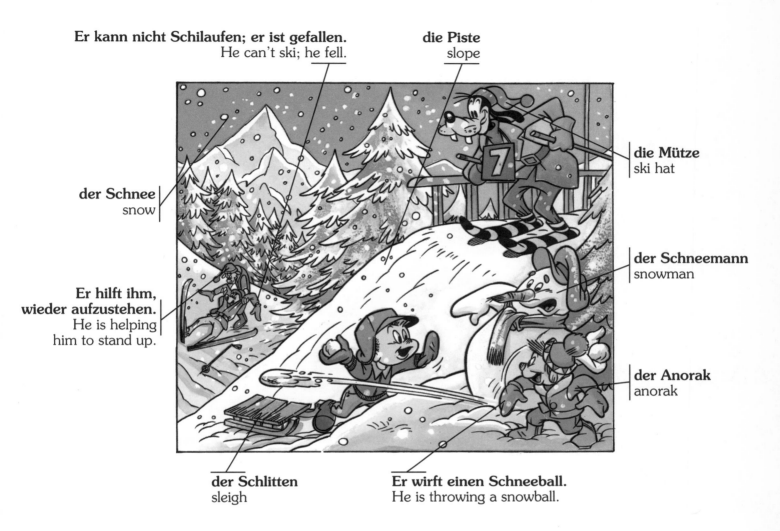

Er kann nicht Schilaufen; er ist gefallen.
He can't ski; he fell.

die Piste
slope

die Mütze
ski hat

der Schnee
snow

der Schneemann
snowman

Er hilft ihm, wieder aufzustehen.
He is helping him to stand up.

der Anorak
anorak

der Schlitten
sleigh

Er wirft einen Schneeball.
He is throwing a snowball.

Es schneit, es ist Winter.
It is snowing; it is winter.

Es ist kalt.
It is cold.

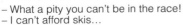

– What a pity you can't be in the race!
– I can't afford skis…

– Starch

– I should have thought of this long ago!

das Fest • holidays

das Weihnachtsfest • Christmas

die Kugel
ball

der Weihnachtsmann
Father Christmas

der Weihnachtsbaum
Christmas tree

der Kamin
fireplace

die Girlande
garland

das Holzscheit
log

Trick bewundert sein Geschenk.
Dewey is admiring his present.

Der Weihnachtsmann ist vorbeigekommen.
Father Christmas has come.

– Here's the turkey, Donald!

– Breast or leg?

das Picknick • the picnic

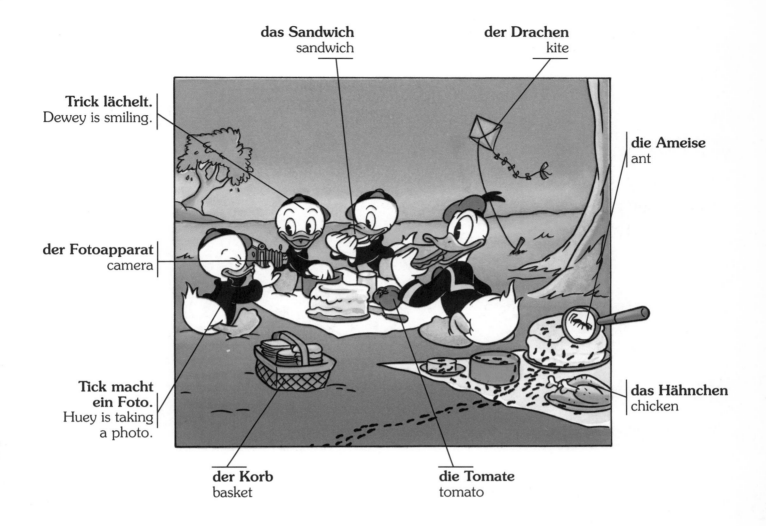

das Sandwich
sandwich

der Drachen
kite

Trick lächelt.
Dewey is smiling.

die Ameise
ant

der Fotoapparat
camera

**Tick macht
ein Foto.**
Huey is taking
a photo.

das Hähnchen
chicken

der Korb
basket

die Tomate
tomato

Das ist ein kaltes Essen.
It is a cold meal.

Es ist Sonntag, alle picknicken, sogar die Ameisen!
It is Sunday; everyone is having a picnic, even the ants!

der Geburtstag • the birthday party

Er gibt ihm einen Bonbon.
He is giving him a sweet.

Er macht Track ein Geschenk.
He is giving Louie a present.

der Orangensaft
orange juice

der Geburtstagskuchen
birthday cake

die Limonade
lemonade

die Tafel Schokolade
bar of chocolate

der Lutscher
lollipop

Tick bläst die Kerzen auf dem Kuchen aus.
Huey is blowing out the candles on the cake.

Die Neffen haben Geburtstag.
It is the nephews' birthday.

– Our guests haven't come yet…
– … for our birthday party.
– May we eat the ice cream?
– No, wait a little bit longer!

– And now…
– … may we…
– … eat it?
– Okay! You can!

– But first of all, you should get changed…

– Invitation.

der Zirkus • the circus

die Kunstreiterin
rider

der Zuschauer
spectator

der Käfig
cage

die Manege
ring

der Clown
clown

der Jongleur
juggler

der Dompteur
tamer

Das ist das Ende der Vorstellung.
It is the end of the performance.

Die Artisten ziehen vorbei.
The performers are parading.

– It's a beautiful flat, on the first floor at the back.
– That won't do. I'm looking for a flat that looks onto the street.
– For rent

– I have to hurry!

– Second floor, overlooking the street… the rent is $ 500 per month.
– It doesn't matter! I'd like to look at it!

– The drawing room… Note this XIVᵗʰ century painting…

Annexes

German verbs conjugations

	Weak verbs	**Strong verbs**
Infinitive	**machen**	**geben**
Participle I	machend	gebend
Participle II	gemacht	gegeben
Imperative	Mach! Machen wir! Macht! Machen Sie!	Gib! Geben wir! Gebt! Geben Sie!
Indicative Present	ich mache du machst er sie } macht es wir machen ihr macht sie machen Sie machen	ich gebe du gibst er sie } gibt es wir geben ihr gebt sie geben Sie geben
Indicative Preterit	ich machte du machtest er sie } machte es wir machten ihr machtet sie machten Sie machten	ich gab du gabst er sie } gab es wir gaben ihr gabt sie gaben Sie gaben
Indicative Perfect	ich habe gemacht du hast gemacht er sie } hat gemacht es wir haben gemacht ihr habt gemacht sie haben gemacht Sie haben gemacht	ich habe gegeben du hast gegeben er sie } hat gegeben es wir haben gegeben ihr habt gegeben sie haben gegeben Sie haben gegeben
Indicative Pluperfect	ich hatte gemacht du hattest gemacht er sie } hatte gemacht es wir hatten gemacht ihr hattet gemacht sie hatten gemacht Sie hatten gemacht	ich hatte gegeben du hattest gegeben er sie } hatte gegeben es wir hatten gegeben ihr hattet gegeben sie hatten gegeben Sie hatten gegeben
Indicative Future	ich werde machen du wirst machen er sie } wird machen es wir werden machen ihr werdet machen sie werden machen Sie werden machen	ich werde geben du wirst geben er sie } wird geben es wir werden geben ihr werdet geben sie werden geben Sie werden geben

Die Zahlen • Numerals

Kardinalzahlen • Cardinal numbers

null	0	nought	siebzig	70	seventy	
eins	1	one	fünfundsiebzig	75	seventy-five	
zwei	2	two	achtzig	80	eighty	
drei	3	three	einundachtzig	81	eighty-one	
vier	4	four	neunzig	90	ninety	
fünf	5	five	einundneunzig	91	ninety-one	
sechs	6	six	(ein)hundert	100	a/one hundred	
sieben	7	seven	(ein)hunderteins	101	a hundred and one	
acht	8	eight	(ein)hundertzwei	102	a hundred and two	
neun	9	nine	(ein)hundertfünfzig	150	a hundred and fifty	
zehn	10	ten	zweihundert	200	two hundred	

			zweihunderteins	201	two hundred and one
			zweihundertzwei	202	two hundred and two
			(ein)tausend	1000	a/one thousand
			(ein)tausendeins	1001	a thousand and one
			(ein)tausendzwei	1002	a thousand and two
			zweitausend	2000	two thousand
			eine Million	1000000	a/one million
			zwei Millionen	2000000	two million

Ordnungszahlen
Ordinal numbers

elf	11	eleven	der/die erste	1.	1st	first
zwölf	12	twelve	der/die zweite	2.	2nd	second
dreizehn	13	thirteen	der/die dritte	3.	3rd	third
vierzehn	14	fourteen	der/die vierte	4.	4th	fourth
fünfzehn	15	fifteen	der/die fünfte	5.	5th	fifth
sechzehn	16	sixteen	der/die sechste	6.	6th	sixth
siebzehn	17	seventeen	der/die sieb(en)te	7.	7th	seventh
achtzehn	18	eighteen	der/die achte	8.	8th	eighth
neunzehn	19	nineteen	der/die neunte	9.	9th	ninth
zwanzig	20	twenty	der/die zehnte	10.	10th	tenth
einundzwanzig	21	twenty-one	der/die elfte	11.	11th	eleventh
zweiundzwanzig	22	twenty-two	der/die zwölfte	12.	12th	twelfth
dreißig	30	thirty	der/die dreizehnte	13.	13th	thirteenth
vierzig	40	forty	der/die vierzehnte	14.	14th	fourteenth
fünfzig	50	fifty	der/die fünfzehnte	15.	15th	fifteenth
sechzig	60	sixty	der/die sechzehnte	16.	16th	sixteenth
			der/die siebzehnte	17.	17th	seventeenth
			der/die achtzehnte	18.	18th	eighteenth
			der/die neunzehnte	19.	19th	nineteenth
			der/die zwanzigste	20.	20th	twentieth
			der/die einundzwanzigste	21.	21st	twenty-first
			der/die zweiundzwanzigste	22.	22nd	twenty-second
			der/die dreißigste	30.	30th	thirtieth

Wieviel Uhr ist es?
What time is it?

4.00	**Es ist vier Uhr.** It is four o'clock.
4.05	**Es ist fünf (Minuten) nach vier.** It is five (minutes) past four.
4.15	**Es ist viertel nach vier.** It is (a) quarter past four.

Es ist zwölf Uhr. / Es ist Mittag.
It is twelve o'clock. / It is noon.

4.30	**Es ist halb fünf.** It is half past four. / It is four thirty.
4.45	**Es ist viertel vor fünf.** It is (a) quarter to five.
4.50	**Es ist zehn (Minuten) vor fünf.** It is ten to five.

Es ist zwölf Uhr. / Es ist Mitternacht.
It is twelve o'clock. / It is midnight.

das Datum • the date

die Tage days			die Monate months	
Montag Monday		*Donnerstag, den 1. Mai 1994* *Thursday, 1ˢᵗ May 1994*	**Januar**	January
Dienstag Tuesday			**Februar**	February
			März	March
Mittwoch Wednesday		*Freitag, den 2. Mai 1994* *Friday, 2ⁿᵈ May 1994*	**April**	April
			Mai	May
Donnerstag Thursday			**Juni**	June
			Juli	July
Freitag Friday		*Samstag, den 3. Mai 1994* *Saturday, 3ʳᵈ May 1994*	**August**	August
			September	September
Samstag Saturday			**Oktober**	October
		Sonntag, den 4. Mai 1994 *Sunday, 4ᵗʰ May 1994*	**November**	November
Sonntag Sunday			**Dezember**	December

Guide to pronunciation
Table of phonetic symbols

Vowels	Consonants

Vowels

[i] **I**dee, bi**e**ten
[y] Ph**y**sik, M**ü**he
[u] M**u**sik, **Uh**r
[e] **e**gal, S**ee**
[ø] **Ö**dem, **Ö**se
[o] T**o**mate, **O**fen
[ɪ] b**i**tten
[ʏ] d**ü**nn
[ʊ] Dr**ü**ck
[ɛ] **ä**ndern, B**ä**r
[œ] **ö**ffnen
[ɔ] **o**ffen
[a] h**a**t
[ə] Alt**e**r

Diphtongs

[aɪ] Am**ei**se, L**ai**b
[aʊ] B**au**m
[ɔʏ] **äu**geln, h**eu**te

Semivowells

[j] **j**a
[aʊ] **W**hisky

Consonants

b] **b**ar
[ç] Ar**ch**e, Köni**g**
[x] au**ch**
[d] **d**u
[f] au**f**, **V**ater
[g] **G**enie
[h] **H**ut, Be**h**älter
[k] **K**ur, Antra**g**, Geschma**ck**
[kv] **Qu**al
[l] **l**eben
[m] a**m**
[n] a**n**
[ŋ] A**ng**st, O**n**kel
[ɲ] Champi**gn**on
[p] a**p**art, a**b**
[r] a**r**m
[s] al**s**, Ki**ss**en, Flu**ß**
[z] Ro**s**e
[ʃ] **sch**wer, **St**raße
[t] al**t**, Han**d**
[v] **w**o
[ts] **Z**immer

Diacriticals signs

[ː] shows that the preceding vowel is long
['] shows the primary stress (stand at the beginning of the stressed syllable)
[ˌ] shows the secondary stress
[ʔ] glottal stop (shows an interruption of the breath stream during speech)

Index

Abbreviations

adj.	adjective
adv.	adverb
f.	feminine
interj.	interjection
inv.	invariable
m.	masculine
n.	noun
nt.	neuter
pl.	plural
v.	verb

German – English

A

Abendessen (-) ['a:bənt,ʔɛsən] *n. nt.* : dinner **57**
Abflug ("e) ['abflu:k] *n. m.* : departure **72**
abholen [ab'ho:lən] *v.* : pick up **37**
Absatz ("e) [ap'zats] *n. m.* : heel **42**
Addieren (Ø) [a'di:rən] *n. nt.* : addition **28**
Adler (-) ['a:dlər] *n. m.* : eagle **60, 61**
Affe (en) ['afə] *n. m.* : monkey **69**
alt [alt] *adj.* : old **36**
Ameise (n) ['a:maɪzə] *n. f.* : ant **91**
Ampel (n) ['ampəl] *n. f.* : (traffic) light **18**
amüsieren [amy'zi:rən] *v.* : have*fun **42**
Ananas (-) ['ananas] *n. f.* : pineapple **53**
andere(r, s) ['andərə] *adj.* : other **76**
Angel (n) ['aŋəl] *n. f.* : fishing rod **64**
angeln ['aŋəln] *v.* : catch***64**
Angler (s) ['aŋlər] *n. m.* : fisherman **64**
Angst haben*['aŋst,ha:bən] : be*afraid **10, 69**
Anker (-) ['aŋkər] *n. m.* : anchor **65**
Ankunft (Ø) ['aŋkʊnft] *n. f.* : arrival **72**
Anorak (s) ['anorak] *n. m.* : anorak **87**
sich **anziehen*** [zɪç'an,tsi:ən] *v.* : get*dressed **40**
Anzug ("e) ['antsu:k] *n. m.* : suit **39, 41**
Apfel (¨) ['apfəl] *n. m.* : apple **53**
applaudieren [aplaʊ'di:rən] *v.* : clap **78**
Aquarium (rien) [a'kva:riʊm] *n. nt.* :
fish bowl **11**
Arbeit (en) ['arbaɪt] *n. f.* : work **52**; job **29**
arbeitslos sein* ['arbaɪts,lo:s,zaɪn] : be*out of work **36**
Arm (e) [arm] *n. m.* : arm **35, 47**
arm [arm] *adj.* : poor **38, 77**
Armband ("er) ['armbant] *n. nt.* : bracelet **43**
Artist (en) [ar'tɪst] *n. m.* : performer **93**
Arzt ("e) [a:rtst] *n. m.* : doctor **49**
Ast ("e) [ast] *n. m.* : branch **60**
atmen ['a:tmən] *v.* : breathe **49**
auch [aʊx] *adv.* : too **75**
aufmachen ['aʊf,maxən] *v.* : open **84**
aufstehen* ['aʊf,ʃte:ən] *v.* : get*up **12**
auf Wiedersehen! [,aʊf'vi:dərze:ən] *interj.* :
bye! **8, 14**
Auge (n) ['aʊgə] *n. nt.* : eye **48, 84**
Augenbraue (n) ['aʊgən,braʊə] *n. f.* : eyebrow **48**
ausgezeichnet ['aʊsgə,tsaɪçnət] *adj.* : excellent **26**
aushalten* ['aʊs,haltən] *v.* : stand***42**
Ausrüstung (en) ['aʊs,rystuŋ] *n. f.* : sportsgear **85**
Aussehen (-) ['aʊs,ze:ən] *n. nt.* : appearance **36**
aussuchen ['aʊs,zu:xən] *v.* : choose***69**

B

Baby (s) ['be:bi] *n. nt.* : baby **35, 48**
Babysitter (-) ['be:bi,zɪtər] *n. m.* : babysitter **37**
Bach ("e) [bax] *n. m.* : brook **62**
Bäcker (-), **in** (nen) ['bɛkər] *n.* : baker **20**
Bäckerei (en) ['bɛkəraɪ] *n. f.* : bakery **20**
Badeanzug ("e) ['ba:də,ʔantsu:k] *n. m.* :
bathing suit **73**
Bademantel (¨) ['ba:də,mantəl] *n. m.* :
bathrobe **15**
baden ['ba:dən] *v.* : have*a bath **15**
Badewanne (n) ['ba:də,vanə] *n. f.* : bath **15**
Badezimmer (-) ['ba:də,tsɪmər] *n. nt.* :
bathroom **15**
Bahnhof ("e) ['ba:nho:f] *n. m.* : station **22**

Bahnsteig (e) ['ba:nʃtaɪk] *n. m.* : platform **22**
bald [balt] *adv.* : soon **12**
Balkon (s) [bal'kõ:] *n. m.* : balcony **9**
Ball ("e) [bal] *n. m.* : ball **75, 85, 86**; dance **39**
Banane (n) [ba'na:nə] *n. f.* : banana **53**
Bank ("e) [baŋk] *n. f.* : bench **81**
Bär (en) [bɛ:r] *n. m.* : bear **30, 38**
Barometer (-) [baro'me:tər] *n. nt.* : barometer **67**
Bart ("e) [ba:rt] *n. m.* : beard **37**
Bauch ("e) [baʊx] *n. m.* : stomach **46**
bauen ['baʊən] *v.* : build***64**
Bauer (n), **Bäuerin** (nen) ['baʊər, 'bɔʏərɪn] *n.* :
farmer **68**
Bauernhof ("e) ['baʊərnho:f] *n. m.* : farm **68**
Bauklotz ("e) ['baʊklɔts] *n. m.* :
building block **75**
Baum ("e) [baʊm] *n. m.* : tree **8, 60, 90**
beaufsichtigen [be'ʔaʊf,zɪçtɪgən] *v.* :
watch (over) **27**
sich **beeilen** [zɪçbe'ʔaɪlən] *v.* : hurry **93**
beibringen* ['baɪ,brɪŋən] *v.* : learn***30**
Bein (e) [baɪn] *n. nt.* : leg **47**
bequem [bə'kve:m] *adj.* : comfortable **11**
berühmt [bə'ry:mt] *adj.* : famous **38**
beschließen* [bə'ʃli:sən] *v.* : decide **68**
besser ['bɛsər] *adv.* : better **72**
beste(r, s) ['bɛstə] *adj.* : best **29**
Bett (en) [bɛt] *n. nt.* : bed **13**
beunruhigt [bə'ʔʊn,ru:ɪkt] *adj.* : worried **49**
bewachen [bə'vaxən] *v.* : guard **68**
bewundern [bə'vʊndərn] *v.* : admire **90**
Biene (n) ['bi:nə] *n. f.* : bee **63**
Bild (er) [bɪlt] *n. nt.* : painting **77**
billig ['bɪlɪç] *adj.* : cheap **21**
Birne (n) ['bɪrnə] *n. f.* : pear **53**
bis bald! [bɪs'balt] *interj.* : see you soon! **8, 22**
blasen* ['bla:zən] *v.* : blow***92**
Blatt ("er) [blat] *n. nt.* : leaf **60**
blau [blaʊ] *adj.* : blue **29**
Bleistift (e) ['blaɪʃtɪft] *n. m.* : pencil **77**
Blitz (e) [blɪts] *n. m.* : lightning **67**
blond [blɔnt] *adj.* : blond **37**
Blume (n) ['blu:mə] *n. f.* : flower **8, 63**
Bluse (n) ['blu:zə] *n. f.* : blouse **39**
Blütenblatt ("er) ['bly:tən,blat] *n. nt.* : petal **63**
Boden (¨) ['bo:dən] *n. m.* : floor **43**
grüne Bohne (n) ['gry:nə,bo:nə] *n. f.* :
green bean **52**
Bonbon (s) [bɔ̃'bɔ̃:] *n. m.* : sweet **28, 92**
Boot (e) [bo:t] *n. nt.* : boat **14**
brauchen ['braʊxən] *v.* : need **36**
braun [braʊn] *adj.* : brown **29**; sun-tanned **73**
braunhaarig ['braʊn,ha:rɪç] *adj.* : dark **37**
Briefmarke (n) ['bri:f,markə] *n. f.* : stamp **21**
Brieftasche (n) ['bri:f,taʃə] *n. f.* : wallet **21**
Briefträger (-) ['bri:f,trɛgər] *n. m.* : postman **18**
Brille (n) ['brɪlə] *n. f.* : glasses *n. pl.* **46**
Brosche (n) ['brɔʃə] *n. f.* : brooch **43**
Brot (e) [bro:t] *n. nt.* : bread **55**
Brücke (n) ['brʏkə] *n. f.* : bridge **64**
Brunnen (-) ['brʊnən] *n. m.* : fountain **81**
Buch ("er) [bu:x] *n. nt.* : book **11, 27, 30**
Bühne (n) ['by:nə] *n. f.* : stage **78**
Bürgersteig (e) ['bʏrgər,ʃtaɪk] *n. m.* :
pavement **18**
Bus (se) [bus] *n. m.* : bus **23**
Busfahrschein (e) ['busfa:r,ʃaɪn] *n. m.* :
bus fare **28**

Bushaltestelle (n) [bus'haltə,ʃtɛlə] *n. f.* :
bus stop **23**
Butter (Ø) ['bʊtər] *n. f.* : butter **55**

C

Campingplatz ("e) ['kɛmpɪŋ,plats] *n. m.* :
camping **74**
Champion (s) ['tʃæmpiən] *n.* : champion **84**
Clown (s) [klaʊn] *n. m.* : clown **93**

D

Dach ("er) [dax] *n. nt.* : roof **9, 68**
Dame (n) ['da:mə] *n. f.* : lady **23, 46**; woman **22**
Damebrett (er) ['da:məbrɛt] *n. nt.* :
draught-board **75**
Damespiel (e) ['da:mə,ʃpi:l] *n. nt.* : checkers
n. pl. **75**
danke! ['daŋkə] *interj.* : thanks! **28, 36**
Decke (n) ['dɛkə] *n. f.* : blanket **12**
denken* ['dɛŋkən] *v.* : think***87**
dick [dɪk] *adj.* : fat **36**
Diplom (e) [di'plo:m] *n. nt.* : diploma **47**
Direktor (en), **in** (nen) [di'rɛktər] *n.* :
headmaster *n. m.* **26**
Dirigent (en) [diri'gɛnt] *n. m.* : conductor **78**
Dividieren [divi'di:rən] *n. nt.* : division **28**
Dollar (s) ['dɔlar] *n. m.* : dollar **28, 47**
Dominostein (e) ['do:mino,ʃtaɪn] *n. nt.* :
domino **75**
Dompteur (e) [dɔmp'tø:r] *n. m.* : tamer **93**
Donner (-) ['dɔnər] *n. m.* : thunder **67**
Drachen (-) ['draxən] *n. m.* : kite **66, 91**
Dreieck (e) ['draɪʔɛk] *n. nt.* : triangle **30**
Dünger (-) ['dʏŋər] *n. m.* : fertilizer **52**
dunkel ['dʊŋkəl] *adj.* : dark **10, 29**
dünn [dʏn] *adj.* : thin **36**
Durcheinander (-) ['dʊrçʔaɪ,nandər] *n. nt.* :
mess **34**
Durst haben* ['dʊrst,ha:bən] : be*thirsty **81**
durstig sein* ['dʊrstɪç,zaɪn] : be*thirsty **54**

E

echt [ɛçt] *adj.* : real **57, 64**
Ei (er) [aɪ] *n. nt.* : egg **55, 60, 61**
Eichhörnchen (-) ['aɪç,hœrnçən] *n. nt.* :
squirrel **60**
einkaufen ['aɪn,kaʊfən] *v.* : shop **20**
einladen ['aɪn,la:dən] *v.* : invite **38**
Einladung (en) ['aɪn,la:dʊŋ] *n. f.* : invitation **92**
einschlafen* ['aɪn,ʃla:fən] *v.* : fall*asleep **62**
einverstanden! ['aɪnfɛr,ʃtandən] *interj.* : okay! **92**
Eis (Ø) [aɪs] *n. nt.* : ice cream **92**
Elefant (en) [ele'fant] *n. m.* : elephant **69**
elegant [ele'gant] *adj.* : smart **39**
elektrisch [e'lɛktrɪʃ] *adj.* : electric **79**
Ellenbogen (-) ['ɛlən,bo:gən] *n. m.* : elbow **47**
Ende (n) ['ɛndə] *n. nt.* : end **93**
endlich ['ɛntlɪç] *adv.* : at last **30, 62**
Ente (n) ['ɛntə] *n. f.* : duck **68**

Entsafter (-) [ɛnt'zaftər] *n. m.* : orange squeezer **36**
Erbse (n) ['ɛrpsə] *n. f.* : pea **52**
Erdbeere (n) ['e:rt,be:rə] *n. f.* : strawberry **53**
Erdkugel (n) ['e:rt,ku:gəl] *n. f.* : globe **30**
Erhöhung (en) [ɛr'hø:ʊŋ] *n. f.* : raise **28**
erklären [ɛr'klɛ:rən] *v.* : explain **63**
Erklärung (en) [ɛr'klɛrʊŋ] *n. f.* : explanation **65**
erstaunlich [ɛr'ʃtaʊnlıç] *adj.* : amazing **69**
erste(r, s) ['ɛrstə] *adj.* : first **40, 93**
Essen (-) ['ɛsən] *n. nt.* : meal **91**
essen * ['ɛsən] *v.* : eat * **54, 56, 60, 77, 92**
Eule (n) ['ɔʏlə] *n. f.* : owl **66**

F

fahren * ['fa:rən] *v.* : drive * **23, 62**
Fahrer (-), **in** (nen) ['fa:rər] *n.* : driver **23**
Fahrgast (¨e) ['fa:rgast] *n. m.* : passenger **23**
Fahrrad (¨er) ['fa:rra:t] *n. nt.* : bicycle **18**; bike **19**
fallen * ['falən] *v.* : fall * **60, 87**
falsch singen * ['falʃ,zıŋən] : sing * out of tune **79**
Familie (n) [fa'mi:liə] *n. f.* : family **34**
fangen * ['faŋən] *v.* : catch * **76**
Farbe (n) ['farbə] *n. f.* : colour **29**
Farbtube (n) ['farp,tu:bə] *n. f.* : tube of paint **77**
Federbett (en) ['fe:dərbɛt] *n. nt.* : eiderdown **13**
Fenster (-) ['fɛnstər] *n. nt.* : window **9**
Fensterladen (¨) ['fɛnstər,la:dən] *n. m.* : shutter **9**
Ferien ['fe:riən] *n. pl.* : holidays **22**
fernsehen ['fɛrnze:ən] *v.* : watch television **11**
Fernseher (-) ['fɛrnze:ər] *n. m.* : television **11**
fesseln ['fɛsəln] *v.* : enthrall **80**
Fest (e) [fɛst] *n. nt.* : holiday **89**
Feuer (-) ['fɔʏər] *n. nt.* : fire **74**
Film (e) [fılm] *n. m.* : film **80**
finden * ['fındən] *v.* : find * **39, 60, 61**
Finger (-) ['fıŋər] *n. m.* : finger **47**
Fisch (e) [fıʃ] *n. m.* : fish **57, 64, 76**
Flasche (n) ['flaʃə] *n. f.* : bottle **56**
Fleck (e) [flɛk] *n. m.* : stain **77**
Fleisch (ø) [flaıʃ] *n. nt.* : meat **56, 74**
Fleischer (-) ['flaıʃər] *n. m.* : butcher **20**
Fleischerei (en) ['flaıʃəraı] *n. f.* : butcher's shop **20**
fleißig sein * ['flaısıç,zaın] : work hard **26**
Fliege (n) ['fli:gə] *n. f.* : bow tie **39**
fliegen * ['fli:gən] *v.* : fly * **62**
fliegende Untertasse ['fli:gəndə,ʊntər,tasə] *f.* : flying saucer **66**
fließen * ['fli:sən] *v.* : flow **64**
Flöte (n) ['flø:tə] *n. f.* : flute **78**
Flügel (-) ['fly:gəl] *n. m.* : breast **90**
Flughafen (¨) ['flu:k,ha:fən] *n. m.* : airport **72**
Flugzeug (e) ['flu:ktsɔʏk] *n. nt.* : (aero)plane **66, 72**
Flugzeughalle (n) ['flu:ktsɔʏk,halə] *n. f.* : hangar **72**
Flur (e) [flu:r] *n. m.* : hall **10**
Fluß (¨sse) [flʊs] *n. m.* : river **64**
Form (en) [fɔrm] *n. f.* : shape **30**
Foto (s) ['fo:to] *n. nt.* : photo **46, 91**
Fotoapparat (e) ['fo:to?apa,ra:t] *n. m.* : camera **91**
ein Foto machen [aın'fo:to,maxən] : take * a photo **46, 91**
Frage (n) ['fra:gə] *n. f.* : question **27**
nach dem Weg fragen [naxdem've:k,fra:gən] : ask for directions **18**
Frau (en) [fraʊ] *n. f.* : woman **35, 72**; wife **34**
Freizeit ['fraıtsaıt] *n. f.* : leisure **71**
Freund (e), **in** (nen) [frɔʏnt] *n.* : friend **27**
froh [fro:] *adj.* : happy **30, 31**; glad **74**
fröhlich ['frø:lıç] *adj.* : happy **15**
Frucht (¨e) [frʊxt] *n. f.* : fruit **53**
früh [fry:] *adv.* : early **62**
Frühling (e) ['fry:lıŋ] *n. m.* : spring **8**
Frühstück (e) ['fry:ʃtʏk] *n. nt.* : breakfast **55**

füllen ['fʏlən] *v.* : stuff **20**
Füllung (en) ['fʏlʊŋ] *n. f.* : stuffing **20**
Fuß (¨e) [fu:s] *n. m.* : foot **42, 47**
Fußboden (¨) ['fu:s,bo:dən] *n. m.* : floor **10**
Fußgänger (-), **in** (nen) ['fu:s,gɛŋər] *n.* : pedestrian **19**

G

Gabel (n) ['ga:bəl] *n. f.* : fork **54**
gähnen ['gɛ:nən] *v.* : yawn **13**
Gang (¨e) [gaŋ] *n. m.* : aisle **80**
Garage (n) [ga'ra:ʒə] *n. f.* : garage **9**
Garten (¨) ['gartən] *n. m.* : garden **8, 69**
Gartenweg (e) ['gartən,ve:k] *n. m.* : path **8**
Gast (¨e) [gast] *n. m.* : guest **40, 92**
Gebäude (-) [gə'bɔʏdə] *n. nt.* : building **18**
geben * ['ge:bən] *v.* : give **92**
Gebirge (-) [gə'bırgə] *n. nt.* : mountain **61**
Gebirgsbach (¨e) [gə'bırgs,bax] *n. m.* : mountain stream **61**
Geburtstag (e) [gə'bu:rts,ta:k] *n. m.* : birthday **92**
Geburtstagsfeier (n) [gə'bu:rts,ta:ks,faıər] *n. f.* : birthday party **92**
gefährlich [gə'fɛ:rlıç] *adj.* : dangerous **62, 85**
gehen * ['ge:ən] *v.* : go * **20, 39, 57, 76**
schlafen gehen * ['ʃla:fən,ge:ən] : go * to bed **75**
Geige (n) ['gaıgə] *n. f.* : violin **78**
Geländer (-) [gə'lɛndər] *n. nt.* : bannisters *n. pl.* **10**
gelb [gɛlp] *adj.* : yellow **29**
Geld (er) [gɛlt] *n. nt.* : money **21**
Geldbeutel (-) ['gɛlt,bɔʏtəl] *n. m.* : purse **21**
Geldschein (e) ['gɛltʃaın] *n. m.* : bank note **21**
Geldstück (e) ['gɛltʃtʏk] *n. nt.* : coin **21**
Gemälde (-) [gə'me:ldə] *n. nt.* : painting **77, 93**
Gemse (n) ['gɛmzə] *n. f.* : chamois **61**
Gemüse (-) [gə'my:zə] *n. nt.* : vegetables *n. pl.* **52**
Gepäck (ø) [gə'pɛk] *n. nt.* : luggage **22**
Geschäft (e) [gə'ʃɛft] *n. nt.* : shop **20**
Geschenk (e) [gə'ʃɛŋk] *n. nt.* : present **90, 92**
das Geschirr spülen [dasgə'ʃır,ʃpy:lən] : do * the dishes **14**
Gesicht (er) [gə'zıçt] *n. nt.* : face **48**
Gesundheit (ø) [gə'zʊnt,haıt] *n. f.* : health **49**
gewinnen * [gə'vınən] *v.* : win * **84, 86**
gießen * ['gi:sən] *v.* : water **8**
Gießkanne (n) ['gi:skanə] *n. f.* : watering can **8**
Gipfel (-) ['gıpfəl] *n. m.* : peak **61**
Giraffe (n) [gi'rafə] *n. f.* : giraffe **69, 76**
Girlande (n) [gır'landə] *n. f.* : garland **90**
Gitarre (n) [gi'tarə] *n. f.* : guitar **74, 79**
glänzen ['glɛntsən] *v.* : glitter **43**
Glas (¨er) [gla:s] *n. nt.* : glass **14, 54**
glatt [glat] *adj.* : straight **37**
glauben ['glaʊbən] *v.* : believe **9**; think * **35, 43**
Gleis (e) [glaıs] *n. nt.* : track **22**
Glück (ø) [glʏk] *n. nt.* : luck **31**
glücklich ['glʏklıç] *adj.* : happy **35**
Gold (ø) [gɔlt] *n. nt.* : gold **43**
Goldfisch (e) ['gɔltfıʃ] *n. m.* : goldfish **11**
Gras (¨er) [gra:s] *n. nt.* : grass **60**
grau [graʊ] *adj.* : grey **29**
grillen ['grılən] *v.* : grill **74**
groß [gro:s] *adj.* : big **42**; tall **36**
Großmutter (¨) ['gro:s,mʊtər] *n. f.* : grandmother **34**
Großvater (¨) ['gro:s,fatər] *n. m.* : grandfather **34**
grün [gry:n] *adj.* : green **18, 29**
Grünpflanze (n) ['gry:n,pflantsə] *n. f.* : green plant **63**
Gürtel (-) ['gʏrtəl] *n. m.* : belt **41**
gut [gu:t] *adj.* : good **29, 79**
gut [gu:t] *adv.* : well **34, 77, 86**
Gymnastik (ø) [gʏm'nastık] *n. f.* : gymnastics *n. pl.* **85**

H

Haar (e) [ha:r] *n. nt.* : hair **35, 37, 48**
Haarspange (n) ['ha:r,ʃpaŋə] *n. f.* : slide **37**
Hafen (¨) ['hafən] *n. m.* : harbour **65**
Hahn (¨e) [ha:n] *n. m.* : cock **68**
Hähnchen (-) ['hɛ:nçən] *n. nt.* : chicken **20, 56, 91**
halbe Stunde ['halbə'ʃtʊndə] *f.* : half an hour **35**
Halbstiefel (-) ['halp,ʃti:fəl] *n. m.* : ankle boot **42**
Hals (¨e) [hals] *n. m.* : neck **46, 69**
Halskette (n) ['hals,kɛtə] *n. f.* : necklace **43**
halten * ['haltən] *v.* : hold * **35**
Hand (¨e) [hant] *n. f.* : hand **47**
Handtuch (¨er) ['hantu:x] *n. nt.* : towel **15**
hängen * ['hɛŋən] *v.* : hang * up **67**
Hanteln ['hantəln] *n. f. pl.* : weights *n. pl.* **85**
Harfe (n) ['harfə] *n. f.* : harp **79**
häßlich ['hɛslıç] *adj.* : ugly **36**
Häuptling (e) ['hɔʏptlıŋ] *n. m.* : chief **38**
Haus (¨er) [haʊs] *n. nt.* : house **7, 9, 10, 67, 68**
Hausaufgaben ['haʊs,aʊf,ga:bən] *n. f. pl.* : homework *n.* **28**
Hausschuh (e) ['haʊsʃu:] *n. m.* : slipper **41**
Hecke (n) ['hekə] *n. f.* : hedge **8**
Heft (e) [hɛft] *n. nt.* : exercise book **28**
Held (e) [hɛlt] *n. m.* : hero **80**
helfen * ['hɛlfən] *v.* : help **28, 87**
hell [hɛl] *adj.* : light **29**
Hemd (en) [hɛmt] *n. nt.* : shirt **41**
Herbst (e) [hɛrpst] *n. m.* : autumn **60**
Herd (e) [he:rt] *n. m.* : cooker **14**
Herr (en) [hɛr] *n. m.* : gentleman **23**
Herz (en) [hɛrts] *n. nt.* : heart **49**
heute ['hɔʏtə] *adv.* : today **27, 60, 72**
heute abend ['hɔʏtə,abent] : tonight **39**
Hilfe (n) ['hılfə] *n. f.* : help **26**
Hilfe! ['hılfə] *interj.* : help! **72**
Himmel (-) ['hıməl] *n. m.* : sky **66**
Hintern (-) ['hıntərn] *n. m.* : bottom **46**
Hirsch (e) [hırʃ] *n. m.* : stag **76**
Hocker (-) ['hɔkər] *n. m.* : stool **14**
Hof (¨e) [ho:f] *n. m.* : playground **27**; back **93**
hoffen ['hɔfən] *v.* : hope **29**
höflich ['hø:flıç] *adj.* : polite **38**
Holz (¨er) [hɔlts] *n. nt.* : wood **74**
Holzscheit (e) ['hɔltsʃaıt] *n. nt.* : log **90**
Honig (e) ['ho:nıç] *n. m.* : honey **55**
Hose (n) ['ho:zə] *n. f.* : trousers *n. pl.* **40**
Huhn (¨er) [hu:n] *n. nt.* : hen **68**
Hühnerstall (¨e) ['hy:nər,ʃtal] *n. m.* : henhouse **68**
Hund (e), **Hündin** (nen) [hʊnt, 'hʏndın] *n.* : dog **68**
Hundehütte (n) ['hʊndə,hʏtə] *n. f.* : kennel **68**
hungrig ['hʊŋrıç] *adj.* : starving **77**
hungrig sein * ['hʊŋrıç,zaın] : be * hungry **54**
hupen ['hu:pən] *v.* : hoot **19**
Hut (¨e) [hu:t] *n. m.* : hat **40, 80**
Hütte (n) ['hʏtə] *n. f.* : chalet **61**

I

Idee (n) [i'de:] *n. f.* : idea **66, 68**
immer ['ımər] *adv.* : always **29**
Indianer (-), **in** (nen) [ındi'a:nər] *n.* : Indian **38, 64**
Instrument (e) [ınstru'mɛnt] *n. nt.* : instrument **79**

J

Jacke (n) ['jakə] *n. f.* : jacket **39**
Jackett (s) [ʒa'kɛt] *n. nt.* : jacket **40**
jagen ['ja:gən] *v.* : hunt **38**
Jahrhundert (e) [ja:r'hʊndərt] *n. nt.* : century **93**
Jeans [dʒi:nz] *n. pl.* : jeans *n. pl.* **40**
jetzt [jɛtst] *adv.* : now **66, 72, 92**
Jongleur (e) [ʒɔ̃'glø:r] *n. m.* : juggler **93**
jung [jʊŋ] *adj.* : young **35**
Junge (n) ['jʊŋə] *n. m.* : boy **35**

K

Kaffee (s) ['kafe] *n. m.* : coffee **55**
Kaffeekanne (n) ['kafe‚kanə] *n. f.* : coffee-pot **55**
Käfig (e) ['kɛːfɪç] *n. m.* : cage **93**
Kalb (¨er) [kalp] *n. nt.* : calf **62**
kalt [kalt] *adj.* : cold **74, 87, 91**
Kamel (e) [ka'meːl] *n. nt.* : camel **76**
Kamin (e) [ka'miːn] *n. m.* : fireplace **90**
Kamm (¨e) [kam] *n. m.* : comb **15**
Känguruh (s) ['kɛŋguru] *n. nt.* : kangaroo **76**
Kaninchen (-) [ka'niːnçən] *n. nt.* : rabbit **62**
Kanu (s) ['kaːnu] *n. nt.* : canoe **64**
kaputtmachen [ka'pʊt‚maxən] *v.* : break * **14**
Karotte (n) [ka'rɔtə] *n. f.* : carrot **52**
Kartoffel (n) [kar'tɔfəl] *n. f.* : potato **52**
Käse (-) ['kɛːzə] *n. m.* : cheese **56**
Kasse (n) ['kasə] *n. f.* : cash register **21**
Kassierer (-), **in** (nen) [ka'siːrər] *n.* : cashier **21**
Kastanie (n) [kas'taːniə] *n. f.* : chestnut **60**
Katze (n) ['katsə] *n. f.* : cat **68**
kaufen ['kaʊfən] *v.* : buy * **9, 21, 52**
Kerze (n) ['kɛrtsə] *n. f.* : candle **92**
Keule (n) ['kɔʏlə] *n. f.* : leg **56, 90**
Kieselstein (e) ['kiːzəl‚ʃtaɪn] *n. m.* : pebble **64**
Kilo (-) ['kiːlo] *n. nt.* : kilo **20**
Kind (er) [kɪnt] *n. nt.* : child **27, 35**
Kinderwagen (-) ['kɪndər‚vaːgən] *n. m.* : pushchair **81**
Kinn (e) [kɪn] *n. nt.* : chin **48**
Kino (s) ['kiːno] *n. nt.* : cinema **80**
Kirsche (n) ['kɪrʃə] *n. f.* : cherry **53**
Kittel (-) ['kɪtəl] *n. m.* : smock **77**
Klasse (n) ['klasə] *n. f.* : class **26**
Klassenzimmer (-) ['klasən‚tsɪmər] *n. nt.* : classroom **26**
Klavier (e) [kla'viːr] *n. nt.* : piano **78**
Kleid (er) [klaɪt] *n. nt.* : dress **39**
Kleiderschrank (¨e) ['klaɪdər‚ʃraŋk] *n. m.* : wardrobe **41**
Kleiderständer (-) ['klaɪdər‚ʃtɛndər] *n. m.* : coatstand **40**; peg **41**
Kleidung (en) ['klaɪdʊŋ] *n. f.* : clothes *n. pl.* **39, 40, 41**
klein [klaɪn] *adj.* : small **36**
klingeln ['klɪŋəln] *v.* : ring * **12**
Knie (-) [kniː] *n. nt.* : knee **47**
Knochen (-) ['knɔxən] *n. m.* : bone **54**
kochen ['kɔxən] *v.* : cook **14**
Kochtopf (¨e) ['kɔxtɔpf] *n. m.* : saucepan **14**
Koffer (-) ['kɔfər] *n. m.* : suitcase **22**
Kohl (e) [koːl] *n. m.* : cabbage **52**
können * ['kœnən] *v.* : can * **80**
konzentrieren [kɔntsɛn'triːrən] *v.* : concentrate **84**
Konzert (e) [kɔn'tsɛrt] *n. nt.* : concert **78, 79**
Kopf (¨e) [kɔpf] *n. m.* : head **46**
Kopfkissen (-) ['kɔpf‚kɪsən] *n. nt.* : pillow **13**
Kopfschmerzen haben * ['kɔpfʃmɛrtsən‚haːbən] : have * a headache **49**
Korb (¨e) [kɔrp] *n. m.* : basket **91**
Körper (-) ['kœrpər] *n. m.* : body **46, 47**
krank [kraŋk] *adj.* : sick **49**
Krankenhaus (¨er) ['kraŋkən‚haʊs] *n. nt.* : hospital **49**
Krankenschwester (n) ['kraŋkənʃvɛstər] *n. f.* : nurse **49**
Krankenwagen (-) ['kraŋkən‚vaːgən] *n. m.* : ambulance **49**
Krawatte (n) [kra'vatə] *n. f.* : tie **39**
Kreis (e) [kraɪs] *n. m.* : circle **30**
Kreuzung (en) ['krɔʏtsʊŋ] *n. f.* : crossroads **18**
Krokodil (e) [kroko'diːl] *n. nt.* : crocodile **69**
Küche (n) ['kʏçə] *n. f.* : kitchen **14, 57**
Kuchen (-) ['kuːxən] *n. m.* : cake **14, 92**
Küchenschrank (¨e) ['kʏçən‚ʃraŋk] *n. m.* : cupboard **14**
Kuckucksuhr (en) ['kʊkʊks‚ʔuːr] *n. f.* : cuckoo clock **31**
Kugel (n) ['kuːgəl] *n. f.* : ball **90**

Kugelschreiber (-) ['kuːgəlʃraɪbər] *n. m.* : pen **28**
Kuh (¨e) [kuː] *n. f.* : cow **62**
Kühlschrank (¨e) ['kyːlʃraŋk] *n. m.* : fridge **57**
Künstler (-), **in** (nen) ['kʏnstlər] *n.* : artist **77**
Kunstreiter (-), **in** (nen) ['kʊnst‚raɪtər] *n.* : rider **93**
Kürbis (sse) ['kʏrbɪs] *n. m.* : pumpkin **52**
kurz [kʊrts] *adj.* : short **37, 40**

L

lächeln ['lɛçəln] *v.* : smile **91**
Laden (¨) ['laːdən] *n. m.* : shop **20**
Laken (-) ['laːkən] *n. nt.* : sheet **12**
Lampe (n) ['lampə] *n. f.* : lamp **12**
Land (¨er) [lant] *n. nt.* : country(side) **62**
landen ['landən] *v.* : land **72**
Landschaft (en) ['lantʃaft] *n. f.* : landscape **62**
lang [laŋ] *adj.* : long **37, 69**
lassen * ['lasən] *v.* : let * **13**; leave * **54**
Lastwagen (-) ['last‚vaːgən] *n. m.* : lorry **23**
Lauch (e) [laʊx] *n. m.* : leek **52**
Lauf (¨e) [laʊf] *n. m.* : race **84**
laufen * ['laʊfən] *v.* : run * **27, 69, 84**
Lebensmittelgeschäft (e) ['leːbəns‚mɪtəlgeʃɛft] *n. nt.* : grocer's shop **20**
lecker ['lɛkər] *adj.* : delicious **56, 60**
leer [leːr] *adj.* : empty **30**
legen ['leːgən] *v.* : put * **27**
Lehrer (-), **in** (nen) ['leːrər] *n.* : (school)teacher **26, 27**
leid tun * ['laɪt‚tuːn] : be * sorry **38**
Leinwand (¨e) ['laɪnvant] *n. f.* : canvas **77**; screen **80**
lernen ['lɛrnən] *v.* : learn * **27**
lesen * ['leːzən] *v.* : read * **11**
leuchten ['lɔʏçtən] *v.* : shine * **66**
Leuchtturm (¨e) ['lɔʏçt‚tʊrm] *n. m.* : lighthouse **65**
Leute ['lɔʏtə] *n. pl.* : people *n.* **33**
Licht (er) [lɪçt] *n. nt.* : light **10**
Lichtung (en) ['lɪçtʊŋ] *n. f.* : clearing **60**
lieben ['liːbən] *v.* : love **8**
liegen * ['liːgən] *v.* : be * lying down **47**
Limonade (n) [limo'naːdə] *n. f.* : lemonade **92**
Lineal (e) [line'aːl] *n. nt.* : ruler **77**
Löffel (-) ['lœfəl] *n. m.* : spoon **54**
Lokomotive (n) [lokomo'tiːvə] *n. f.* : engine **22**
los sein * ['loːszaɪn] : happen **76**
Lösung (en) ['løːzʊŋ] *n. f.* : solution **55**
Löwe (n), **Löwin** (nen) ['løːvə] *n.* : lion **69**
Lutscher (-) ['lʊtʃər] *n. m.* : lollipop **92**

M

Mädchen (-) ['mɛːtçən] *n. nt.* : girl *n. f.* **23, 35, 37, 39**
malen ['maːlən] *v.* : paint **77**
Manege (n) [ma'neːʒə] *n. f.* : ring **93**
Mann (¨er) [man] *n. m.* : man **35**; husband **34**
Mantel (¨) ['mantəl] *n. m.* : coat **40**
Margerite (n) [margə'riːtə] *n. f.* : daisy **63**
Marmelade (n) [marmə'laːdə] *n. f.* : jam **55**
Masseur (e), **in** (nen) [ma'søːr] *n.* : masseur, euse **47**
Matratze (n) [ma'tratsə] *n. f.* : mattress **12**
Mauer (n) ['maʊər] *n. f.* : wall **9**
Medaille (n) [me'daljə] *n. f.* : medal **84**
Medizin (en) [medi'tsiːn] *n. f.* : medicine **14, 49**
Meer (e) [meːr] *n. nt.* : sea **65**
Meisterwerk (e) ['maɪstər‚vɛrk] *n. nt.* : masterpiece **77**
menschlich ['mɛnʃlɪç] *adj.* : human **45**
Messer (-) ['mɛsər] *n. nt.* : knife **54**
mieten ['miːtən] *v.* : rent **9**
Mikro (s) ['mikro] *n. nt.* : microphone **79**
Milch (∅) [mɪlç] *n. f.* : milk **21, 55**
Minute (n) [mi'nuːtə] *n. f.* : minute **31**

Mittagessen (-) ['mɪta:k‚ʔɛsən] *n. nt.* : lunch **56**
Mobile (s) [mo'biːlə] *n. nt.* : mobile **75**
mögen * ['møːgən] *v.* : like **57**
Mole (n) ['moːlə] *n. f.* : jetty **65**
Monat (e) ['moːnat] *n. m.* : month **93**
Mond (e) [moːnt] *n. m.* : moon **66**
Morgen (-) ['mɔrgən] *n. m.* : morning **52, 62**
morgen ['mɔrgən] *adv.* : tomorrow **31, 52**
Morgenmantel (¨) ['mɔrgən‚mantəl] *n. m.* : dressing gown **13**
Motorrad (¨er) [mo'toːr‚rat] *n. nt.* : motorcycle **23**
Motte (n) ['mɔtə] *n. f.* : moth **41**
Möwe (n) ['møːvə] *n. f.* : seagull **66**
müde ['myːdə] *adj.* : tired **13**
Mülleimer (-) ['mʏl‚ʔaɪmər] *n. m.* : dustbin **14**
Multiplizieren (∅) [mʊltipli'tsiːrən] *n. nt.* : multiplication **28**
Mund (¨er) [mʊnt] *n. m.* : mouth **48**
Murmel (n) ['mʊrməl] *n. f.* : marble **27**
Muschel (n) ['mʊʃəl] *n. f.* : shell **73**
Museum (seen) [mu'zeːʊm] *n. nt.* : museum **61**
Musik (en) [mu'ziːk] *n. f.* : music **78, 79**
Musiker (-), **in** (nen) [mu'ziːkər] *n.* : musician **79**
muskulös ['mʊskulœz] *adj.* : muscled **47**
Müsli (s) ['myzli] *n. nt.* : cereal **55**
Mutter (¨) ['mʊtər] *n. f.* : mother **34**
Mutti (s) ['mʊti] *n. f.* : mother **35**
Mütze (n) ['mʏtsə] *n. f.* : cap **41**

N

Nacht (¨e) [naxt] *n. f.* : night **66**
Nachtmütze (n) ['naxt‚mʏtsə] *n. f.* : nightcap **13**
Nachttisch (e) ['naxt‚tɪʃ] *n. m.* : bedside table **12**
Nahrung (∅) ['naːrʊŋ] *n. f.* : food **51**
naß [nas] *adj.* : wet **67**
Natur (en) [na'tuːr] *n. f.* : nature **59**
Nebel (-) ['neːbəl] *n. m.* : fog **62**
Neffe (n) ['nɛfə] *n. m.* : nephew **55, 92**
Nelke (n) ['nɛlkə] *n. f.* : carnation **63**
auf die Nerven gehen * [aʊfdiː'nɛrfən‚geːən] : drive * mad **11**
Nest (er) [nɛst] *n. nt.* : nest **60**
nett [nɛt] *adj.* : nice **38**
Netz (e) [nɛts] *n. nt.* : net **86**
neu [nɔʏ] *adj.* : new **39, 69**
Nichte (n) ['nɪçtə] *n. f.* : niece **37**
niedlich ['niːtlɪç] *adj.* : cute **48**
Nilpferd (e) ['niːlpfeːrt] *n. nt.* : hippopotamus **69**

O

Obst (∅) [oːpst] *n. nt.* : fruit **53**
Obsttorte (n) ['oːbst‚tɔrtə] *n. f.* : tart **56**
Ofen (¨) ['oːfən] *n. m.* : oven **14**
Ohr (en) [oːr] *n. nt.* : ear **48**
Ohrring (e) ['oːr‚rɪŋ] *n. m.* : earring **43**
Omelett (s) [ɔm(ə)'lɛt] *n. nt.* : omelet **60**
Onkel (-) ['ɔŋkəl] *n. m.* : uncle **14, 34**
Orange (n) [o'rãːʒə] *n. f.* : orange **53, 92**
orange [o'rãːʒə] *adj.* : orange **29**
Orchester (-) [ɔr'kɛstər] *n. nt.* : orchestra **78**

P

Paket (e) [pa'keːt] *n. nt.* : parcel **19**
Palette (n) [pa'lɛtə] *n. f.* : palette **77**
Palme (n) ['palmə] *n. f.* : palm tree **73**
Papier (e) [pa'piːr] *n. nt.* : paper **77**
Paprika (s) ['paprika] *n. m.* : sweet pepper **52**
Park (s) [park] *n. m.* : park **81**
parken ['parkən] *v.* : park **18**
Parkplatz (¨e) ['parkplats] *n. m.* : car park **18**
Partie (n) [par'tiː] *n. f.* : game **75**
Paß (¨sse) [pas] *n. m.* : passport **72**
Pause (n) ['paʊzə] *n. f.* : playtime **27**

Perle (n) ['pɛrlə] *n. f.* : bead **43**
Persönlichkeit (en) [pɛr'zøːnlɪçkaɪt] *n. f.* : personality **38**
Pfanne (n) ['pfanə] *n. f.* : frying pan **57**
Pfeffer (ø) ['pfɛfər] *n. m.* : pepper **54**
Pferd (e) ['pfeːrt] *n. nt.* : horse **68**
Pferdeschwanz (ë) ['pfɛrdə.ʃvants] *n. m.* : ponytail **37**
Pfirsich (e) ['pfɪrzɪç] *n. m.* : peach **53**
Pflanze ['pflantsə] *n. f.* : plant **52, 63**
pflanzen ['pflantsən] *v.* : plant **8**
pflegen ['pfleːgən] *v.* : look after **49**
Pfütze (n) ['pfʏtsə] *n. f.* : puddle **67**
Picknick (s) ['pɪknɪk] *n. nt.* : picnic **91**
Pilz (e) ['pɪlts] *n. m.* : mushroom **60**
Pinguin (e) ['pɪŋguin] *n. m.* : penguin **76**
Pinsel (-) ['pɪnzəl] *n. m.* : paint brush **77**
Piste (n) ['pɪstə] *n. f.* : slope **87**
Platte (n) ['platə] *n. f.* : dish **54, 56**; record **37**
Podium (dien) ['poːdiʊm] *n. nt.* : podium **84**
Polizei (ø) [poli'tsaɪ] *n. f.* : police **65**
Polizist (en) [poli'tsɪst] *n. m.* : policeman **18**
Pony (s) ['poni] *n. m.* : fringe **37**
Porträt (s) [pɔr'trɛː] *n. nt.* : portrait **77**
Post (ø) [pɔst] *n. f.* : post office **18**
praktisch ['praktɪʃ] *adj.* : practical **55**
Preis (e) [praɪs] *n. m.* : price **9**
Projektor (en) [pro'jɛktɔr] *n. m.* : projector **80**
Publikum (ø) ['puːblikʊm] *n. nt.* : audience **78**
Pullover (-) [pʊ'loːvər] *n. m.* : pullover **41**
Pumps (-) [pœmps] *n. m.* : court shoe **42**
Puppe (n) ['pʊpə] *n. f.* : doll **9, 75**
Pute (n) ['puːtə] *n. f.* : turkey **90**
putzen ['pʊtsən] *v.* : clean up **34**
sich die Zähne **putzen** [zɪçdi'tsɛːnə.pʊtsən] : brush one's teeth **15**
Puzzle (s) ['pazl] *n. nt.* : puzzle **75**

Q

Quadrat (e) [kva'draːt] *n. nt.* : square **30**

R

Radiergummi (s) [ra'diːr.gʊmi] *n. m.* : rubber **77**
Radieschen (-) [ra'diːsçən] *n. nt.* : radish **52**
Rasen (-) ['raːzən] *n. m.* : lawn **8**
Rasenmäher (-) ['raːzən.mɛːər] *n. m.* : lawn mower **8**
Rauch (ø) [raʊx] *n. m.* : smoke **74**
Rechen (-) ['rɛçən] *n. m.* : rake **8**
Rechnen (ø) ['rɛçnən] *n. nt.* : arithmetic **28**
Rechteck (e) ['rɛçtʔɛk] *n. nt.* : rectangle **30**
Regal (e) [re'gaːl] *n. nt.* : shelf **14**
Regen (-) ['reːgən] *n. m.* : rain **52, 67**
Regenmantel (ˮ) ['reːgən.mantəl] *n. m.* : raincoat **40, 67**
Regenschirm (e) ['reːgən.ʃɪrm] *n. m.* : umbrella **67**
regnen ['reːgnən] *v.* : rain **52**
Reh (e) [reː] *n. nt.* : deer *n. inv.* **61**
reich [raɪç] *adj.* : rich **38**
reif [raɪf] *adj.* : ripe **53**
Reifen (-) ['raɪfən] *n. m.* : tyre **19**
reinlich ['raɪnlɪç] *adj.* : clean **15**
Reis (ø) [raɪs] *n. m.* : rice **56**
reiten* ['raɪtən] *v.* : ride* a horse **68**
Rennbahn (en) ['rɛnbaːn] *n. f.* : track **84**
Richtung (en) ['rɪçtʊŋ] *n. f.* : direction **23**
Ring (e) [rɪŋ] *n. m.* : ring **43**
Rock (ë) [rɔk] *n. m.* : skirt **40**
rollen ['rɔlən] *v.* : roll **43**
Rollschuh (e) ['rɔlʃuː] *n. m.* : roller skate **85**
rosa ['roːza] *adj. inv.* : pink **29**
Rose (n) ['roːzə] *n. f.* : rose **63**
rot [roːt] *adj.* : red **29**
rothaarig ['roːt.haːrɪç] *adj.* : red-haired **37**
Rubin (e) [ru'biːn] *n. m.* : ruby **43**

Rücken (-) ['rʏkən] *n. m.* : back **46**
Rucksack (ë) ['rʊkzak] *n. m.* : rucksack **74**
rund [rʊnt] *adj.* : round **30**
die Stirn **runzeln** [diːʃtɪrn.rʊntsəln] : frown **46**
Rutschbahn (en) ['rʊtʃbaːn] *n. f.* : slide **81**
rutschen ['rʊtʃən] *v.* : slide* **81**

S

Saft (ë) [zaft] *n. m.* : juice **92**
sagen ['zaːgən] *v.* : say* **42**; tell* **52**
Sahne (ø) ['zaːnə] *n. f.* : cream **14**
Salat (e) [za'laːt] *n. m.* : lettuce **52**
Salz (e) [zalts] *n. m.* : salt **54**
Sand (e) [zant] *n. m.* : sand **73**
Sandale (n) [zan'daːlə] *n. f.* : sandal **47**
Sandburg (en) ['zantbʊrk] *n. f.* : sand castle **73**
Sandwich (es) ['sɛndwɪtʃ] *n. nt.* : sandwich **91**
Sänger (-), **in** (nen) ['zɛŋər] *n.* : singer **79**
Saxophon (e) [zakso'foːn] *n. nt.* : saxophone **79**
Schachspiel (e) ['ʃax.ʃpiːl] *n. nt.* : chess **75**
Schaffner (-), **in** (nen) ['ʃafnər] *n.* : ticket collector **22**
Schaufel (n) ['ʃaʊfəl] *n. f.* : shovel **8**
Schaukel (n) ['ʃaʊkəl] *n. f.* : swing **81**
Schauspieler (-), **in** (nen) ['ʃaʊ.ʃpiːlər] *n.* : actor, actress **80**
Schein (e) [ʃaɪn] *n. m.* : appearances *n. pl.* **27**
scheinen* ['ʃaɪnən] *v.* : shine* **73**
Scheinwerfer (-) ['ʃaɪn.vɛrfər] *n. m.* : headlight **19**
Schi (er) [ʃiː] *n. m.* : ski **87**
Schiedsrichter (-) ['ʃiːts.rɪçtər] *n. m.* : umpire **86**
Schifahren ['ʃiː.faːrən] *n. nt.* : skiing **87**
Schiff (e) [ʃɪf] *n. nt.* : ship **65**
Schi laufen* ['ʃiː.laʊfən] *v.* : ski **87**
Schild (er) [ʃɪlt] *n. nt.* : road sign **23**
Schimütze (n) ['ʃiː.mʏtsə] *n. f.* : ski hat **87**
Schirmmütze (n) ['ʃɪrm.mʏtsə] *n. f.* : cap **40**
Schlafanzug (ë) ['ʃlaːf.antsuːk] *n. m.* : pyjamas **13**
schlafen* ['ʃlaːfən] *v.* : sleep* **13, 74**
schlafen gehen* ['ʃlaːfən.geːən] : go* to bed **75**
Schlafsack (ë) ['ʃlaːfzak] *n. m.* : sleeping bag **74**
Schlafwandler (-) ['ʃlaːf.vandlər] *n. m.* : sleepwalker **57**
Schlafzimmer (-) ['ʃlaːf.tsɪmər] *n. nt.* : bedroom **12**
schlagen* ['ʃlaːgən] *v.* : ring* **31**
Schläger (-) ['ʃlɛːgər] *n. m.* : bat **86**
Schlagzeug (e) ['ʃlaːktsɔyk] *n. nt.* : drums *n. pl.* **79**
Schlange (n) ['ʃlaŋə] *n. f.* : snake **69**
Schlitten (-) ['ʃlɪtən] *n. m.* : sleigh **87**
Schloß (ˮsser) [ʃlɔs] *n. nt.* : lock **9**
Schlüssel (-) ['ʃlʏsəl] *n. m.* : key **9**
Schlußverkauf (ë) ['ʃlʊsfɛr.kaʊf] *n. m.* : sale **31**
schmal [ʃmaːl] *adj.* : narrow **10**
Schmetterling (e) ['ʃmɛtərlɪŋ] *n. m.* : butterfly **85**
Schmetterlingsnetz (e) ['ʃmɛtərlɪŋs.nɛts] *n. nt.* : butterfly net **85**
Schmuck (ø) [ʃmʊk] *n. m.* : jewellery **43**
schmutzig ['ʃmʊtsɪç] *adj.* : dirty **15**
Schnee (ø) [ʃneː] *n. m.* : snow **87**
Schneeball ['ʃneːbal] *n. m.* : snowball **87**
Schneemann (ˮer) ['ʃneːman] *n. m.* : snowman **87**
schneiden* ['ʃnaɪdən] *v.* : cut* **35**
schneien ['ʃnaɪən] *v.* : snow **87**
schnell [ʃnɛl] *adv.* : quickly **69**
Schnurrbart (ˮe) ['ʃnʊrbaːrt] *n. m.* : moustache **37**
Schnürsenkel (-) ['ʃnyːrs.ɛŋkəl] *n. m.* : shoelace **42**
Schokolade (n) [ʃoko'laːdə] *n. f.* : chocolate **92**
schön [ʃøːn] *adj.* : beautiful **62, 93**; lovely **9, 31, 39, 53**
Schornstein (e) ['ʃɔrnʃtaɪn] *n. m.* : chimney **9**
Schrank (ˮe) [ʃraŋk] *n. m.* : wardrobe **12**
schreiben* ['ʃraɪbən] *v.* : write* **26**

Schreibtisch (e) ['ʃraɪptɪʃ] *n. m.* : desk **26**
schreien* ['ʃraɪən] *v.* : scream **80**
Schublade (n) ['ʃuːplaːdə] *n. f.* : drawer **41**
Schuh (e) [ʃuː] *n. m.* : shoe **42, 67**
Schule (n) ['ʃuːlə] *n. f.* : school **25, 26, 27, 30**
Schüler (-), **in** (nen) ['ʃyːlər] *n.* : pupil **26**
Schulranzen (-) ['ʃuːl.rantsən] *n. m.* : satchel **28**
Schulter (n) ['ʃʊltər] *n. f.* : shoulder **46**
Schwamm (ˮe) ['ʃvam] *n. m.* : sponge **14**
schwarz [ʃvarts] *adj.* : black **29**
schweigen* ['ʃvaɪgən] *v.* : keep* one's mouth shut **38**
Schwein (e) [ʃvaɪn] *n. nt.* : pig **62, 68**
schwer [ʃveːr] *adj.* : heavy **22**
schwimmen* ['ʃvɪmən] *v.* : swim* **65, 68**
Schwimmring (e) ['ʃvɪmrɪŋ] *n. m.* : rubber ring **73**
Segel (-) ['zeːgəl] *n. nt.* : sail **65**
sehen* ['zeːən] *v.* : see* **34, 46, 53, 56, 67, 76, 80**
sehr [zeːr] *adv.* : very **39, 62**
Seife (n) ['zaɪfə] *n. f.* : soap **15**
sein* [zaɪn] *v.* : be* **21, 35, 85**
Seite (n) ['zaɪtə] *n. f.* : page **26**
Sekunde (n) [ze'kʊndə] *n. f.* : second **31**
seltsam ['zɛltzam] *adj.* : strange **42**
Serviette (n) [zɛrvi'ɛtə] *n. f.* : napkin **54**
Sessel (-) ['zɛsəl] *n. m.* : armchair **11**; seat **80**
Shampoo (s) ['ʃam'puː] *n. nt.* : shampoo **15**
Shorts [ʃɔrts] *n. pl.* : shorts *n. pl.* **85**
sicher ['zɪçər] *adj.* : sure **20**
Sieger (-) ['ziːgər] *n. m.* : winner **84**
singen* ['zɪŋən] : sing* **79**
sinken* ['zɪŋkən] *v.* : sink* **64**
sitzen* ['zɪtsən] *v.* : be* sitting down **11**
Skateboard (s) ['skeɪtbɔːd] *n. nt.* : skate board **85**
Smaragd (e) [sma'rakt] *n. m.* : emerald **43**
Socke (n) ['zɔkə] *n. f.* : sock **41**
Sohn (ë) [zoːn] *n. m.* : son **34**
Sommer (-) ['zɔmər] *n. m.* : summer **73**
Sonne (n) ['zɔnə] *n. f.* : sun **62, 73**
Sonnenbrille (n) ['zɔnən.brɪlə] *n. f.* : sunglasses *n. pl.* **73**
Sonnenschirm (e) ['zɔnən.ʃɪrm] *n. m.* : beach umbrella **73**
Spaß haben* ['ʃpaːs.haːbən] : have* fun **27, 75**
spät [ʃpɛːt] *adv.* : late **13, 29**
Spiegel (-) ['ʃpiːgəl] *n. m.* : mirror **15**
Spiel (e) [ʃpiːl] *n. nt.* : game **75, 86**
spielen ['ʃpiːlən] *v.* : play **27, 75, 78, 85, 86**
Spieler (-), **in** (nen) ['ʃpiːlər] *n.* : player **86**
Spielsache (n) ['ʃpiːl.zaxə] *n. f.* : toys *n. pl.* **75**
Spielzimmer (-) ['ʃpiːl.tsɪmər] *n. nt.* : playroom **75**
Sport (e) [ʃpɔrt] *n. m.* : sport **83**
Sporthalle (n) ['ʃpɔrt.halə] *n. f.* : gym **85**
Sportplatz (ë) ['ʃpɔrtplats] *n. m.* : stadium **84**
Sportschuh (e) ['ʃpɔrtʃuː] *n. m.* : tennis shoe **42**
Sprengstoff (e) ['ʃprɛŋ.ʃtɔf] *n. m.* : dynamite **19**
springen* ['ʃprɪŋən] *v.* : jump **76, 84**
Spritze (en) ['ʃprɪtsə] *n. f.* : injection **49**; syringe **49**
Spüle (n) ['ʃpyːlə] *n. f.* : sink **14**
das Geschirr **spülen** [dasgə'ʃɪr.ʃpyːlən] : do* the dishes **14**
Spur (en) [ʃpuːr] *n. f.* : track **30**
stabil [ʃta'biːl] *adj.* : sturdy **64**
Stadt (ë) [ʃtat] *n. f.* : town **17, 29**
Stamm (ë) [ʃtam] *n. m.* : trunk **60**
stark [ʃtark] *adj.* : strong **36, 85**
Stärke (n) ['ʃtɛrkə] *n. f.* : starch **87**
starten ['ʃtartən] *v.* : take* off **72**
Stau (e) [ʃtaʊ] *n. m.* : traffic jam **18, 19**
stehen* ['ʃteːən] *v.* : be* standing up **47**
Stengel (-) ['ʃtɛŋəl] *n. m.* : stem **63**
sterben* ['ʃtɛrbən] *v.* : die* **63**
Stereoanlage (n) [ʃte'reoan.laːgə] *n. f.* : stereo **11**
Stern (e) [ʃtɛrn] *n. m.* : star **66**
Stewardeß (ssen) ['ʃtjuːərdɛs] *n. f.* : air hostess **72**
Stiefel (-) ['ʃtiːfəl] *n. m.* : boot **42**
Stirn (en) [ʃtɪrn] *n. f.* : forehead **48**
Stock (ë) ['ʃtɔk] *n. m.* : floor **93**

Strand (¨e) [ʃtrant] *n. m.* : beach **73**
Straße (n) ['ʃtraːsə] *n. f.* : street **18, 93**
Strauß (¨e) [ʃtraʊs] *n. m.* : bouquet **63**
Strauß (e) [ʃtraʊs] *n. m.* : ostrich **76**
Streifen (-) ['ʃtraɪfən] *n. m.* : stripe **29**
Strumpfhose (n) ['ʃtrʊmpf͜hoːzə] *n. f.* : tights
  n. pl. **39**
Stufe (n) ['ʃtuːfə] *n. f.* : step **10**
Stuhl (¨e) [ʃtuːl] *n. m.* : chair **54**
Stunde (n) ['ʃtʊndə] *n. f.* : hour **31, 35**
Sturm (¨e) [ʃtʊrm] *n. m.* : storm **67**
Subtrahieren (Ø) [zʊptra'hiːrən] *n. nt.* :
  subtraction **28**
suchen ['zuːxən] *v.* : look for **93**
Summe (n) ['zʊmən] *n. f.* : total **28**
Supermarkt (¨e) ['zuːpər‚markt] *n. m.* :
  supermarket **20**
Suppe (n) ['zʊpə] *n. f.* : soup **57**
Suppenkelle (n) ['zʊpən‚kɛlə] *n. f.* : ladle **57**
Suppenschüssel ['zʊpən‚ʃysəl] *n. f.* :
  soup tureen **57**
Synthesizer (-) ['sɪnθɪsaɪzər] *n. m.* :
  synthesizer **79**

T

Tafel (n) ['taːfəl] *n. f.* : blackboard **26**
Tag (e) [taːk] *n. m.* : day **68**
Tal (¨er) [taːl] *n. nt.* : valley **61**
Tanne (-) ['tanə] *n. f.* : fir tree **64**
Tante (n) ['tantə] *n. f.* : aunt **34**
tanzen ['tantsən] *v.* : dance **79**
Tapete (n) [ta'peːtə] *n. f.* : wallpaper **69**
tapezieren [tape'tsiːrən] *v.* : paper **69**
Taschengeld ['taʃən‚gɛlt] *n. nt.* : pocket money **28**
Tasse (n) ['tasə] *n. f.* : cup **55**
Taxi (s) ['taksi] *n. nt.* : taxi **23**
Teddybär (en) ['tɛdi‚bɛːr] *n. m.* : teddy bear **75**
Tee (s) [teː] *n. m.* : tea **55**
Teekanne (n) ['teː‚kanə] *n. f.* : teapot **55**
Teich (e) [taɪç] *n. m.* : pond **68**
Teil (e) [taɪl] *n. m.* : part **47**
Telefon (e) [tele'foːn] *n. nt.* : telephone **11**
telefonieren [telefoni:rən] *v.* : make* a
  telephone call **19**
Telefonzelle (n) [tele'foːn‚tsɛlə] *n. f.* :
  telephone kiosk **19**
Teller (-) ['tɛlər] *n. m.* : plate **14, 54**
Teppich (e) ['tɛpɪç] *n. m.* : rug **12**
teuer ['tɔʏər] *adj.* : expensive **21, 77**
Theke (n) ['teːkə] *n. f.* : counter **21**
tief [tiːf] *adj.* : deep **64**
Tier (e) [tiːr] *n. nt.* : animal **68, 69, 76**
Tintenfaß (¨er) ['tɪntən‚fas] *n. nt.* : inkwell **30**
Tisch (e) [tɪʃ] *n. m.* : table **54**
Tischdecke (n) ['tɪʃ‚dɛkə] *n. f.* : tablecloth **56**
Tischtennis (Ø) ['tɪʃ‚tɛnɪs] *n. nt.* : table tennis **86**
Tochter (¨) ['tɔxtər] *n. f.* : daughter **34**
Tomate (n) [to'maːtə] *n. f.* : tomato **91**
Torero (s) [to'rero] *n. m.* : bullfighter **40**
tragen * ['traːgən] *v.* : wear* **39, 46**
Trainingsanzug (¨e) ['trɛːnɪŋs‚antsuːk] *n. m.* :
  tracksuit **41**
Traube (n) ['traʊbə] *n. f.* : grape **53**
Treppe (n) ['trɛpə] *n. f.* : stairs *n. pl.* **10**
treu [trɔʏ] *adj.* : faithful **68**
Trikot (s) [tri'koː] *n. m.* : vest **85**
trinken * ['trɪŋkən] *v.* : drink* **55**
Trompete (n) [trɔm'peːtə] *n. f.* : trumpet **78**
T-Shirt (s) ['tiː‚ʃəːt] *n. nt.* : tee-shirt **41**
Tulpe (n) ['tʊlpə] *n. f.* : tulip **63**
Tür (en) [tyːr] *n. f.* : door **9**

U

über die Straße gehen * [‚yːbərdi'ʃtraːsə‚geːən] :
  cross (the street) **19**

Überraschung (en) [‚yːbər'raʃʊŋ] *n. f.* :
  surprise **14, 38**
Ufer (-) ['uːfər] *n. nt.* : bank **64**
Uhr (en) [uːr] *n. f.* : watch **31, 48**; clock **22**
Uhrzeit (en) ['uːrtsaɪt] *n. f.* : time **31**
umziehen * ['ʊm‚tsiːən] *v.* : get* changed **92**
unmöglich ['ʊnmøːklɪç] *adj.* : impossible **9**
unruhig ['ʊn‚ruːɪç] *adj.* : hectic **66**
Unterrock (¨e) ['ʊntər‚rɔk] *n. m.* : petticoat **39**
Urlaub (e) ['uːrlaʊp] *n. m.* : holidays *n. pl.* **73**

V

Vase (n) ['vaːzə] *n. f.* : vase **11**
Vater (¨) ['faːtər] *n. m.* : father **34**
verblüht [fɛr'blyːt] *adj.* : wilted **63**
vergessen * [fɛr'gɛsən] *v.* : forget* **22, 41, 84**
verkaufen [fɛr'kaʊfən] *v.* : sell* **9, 21**
Verkäufer (-), **in** (nen) [fɛr'kɔʏfər] *n.* :
  salesperson **21**
Verkehr (Ø) [fɛr'keːr] *n. m.* : traffic **19**
Verkehrsmittel (-) [fɛr'keːrs‚mɪtəl] *n. nt.* :
  transport **23**
vermieten [fɛr'miːtən] *v.* : rent **9, 93**
sich verrechnen [zɪç‚fɛr'rɛçnən] *v.* : make* a
  mistake **28**
sich verspäten [zɪç‚fɛr'ʃpɛːtən] *v.* : be* late **22**
sich verstecken [zɪç‚fɛr'ʃtɛkən] *v.* : hide* **76**
verstehen * [fɛr'ʃteːən] *v.* : understand* **30**
versuchen * [fɛr'zuːxən] *v.* : try* **65**
sich verteidigen [zɪç‚fɛr'taɪdigən] *v.* :
  fight* back **80**
verursachen [fɛr'ʔuːr‚zaxən] *v.* : cause **19**
Vetter (n) ['fɛtər] *n. m.* : cousin **34, 36**
viel [fiːl] *adj.* : a lot (of) **41**
viel [fiːl] *adv.* : a lot **56**
vielleicht [fi'laɪçt] *adv.* : perhaps **49**
violett [vio'let] *adj.* : purple **29**
Vogel (¨) ['foːgəl] *n. m.* : bird **61, 62**
voll [fɔl] *adj.* : full **30**
vorbeiziehen * [fɔr'baɪ‚tsiːən] *v.* : parade **93**
Vorstellung (en) ['fɔr‚ʃtɛlʊŋ] *n. f.* :
  performance **93**

W

wachsen * ['vaksən] *v.* : grow* **52**
wach werden * ['vax‚veːrdən] : wake* up **12**
Wagen (-) ['vaːgən] *n. m.* : car **18, 19**; carriage **22**
Wald (¨er) [valt] *n. m.* : forest **60**
Walkie-talkie (s) ['wɔːkɪ‚tɔːkɪ] *n. nt.* :
  walkie-talkie **61**
Wange (n) ['vaŋə] *n. f.* : cheek **48**
sich wärmen [zɪç'vɛrmən] *v.* : warm oneself **74**
warten ['vartən] *v.* : wait (for) **23, 60, 62, 69, 92**
Waschbecken (-) ['vaʃ‚bɛkən] *n. nt.* :
  hand basin **15**
sich waschen * [zɪç'vaʃən] *v.* : wash oneself **15**
Wasser (-) ['vasər] *n. nt.* : water **57**
Wasserhahn (¨e) ['vasər‚haːn] *n. m.* : tap **15**
Wasserschi fahren * ['vasər‚ʃiː‚faːrən] :
  water-ski **65**
Wechselgeld (er) ['vɛksəl‚gɛlt] *n. nt.* : change **21**
wechseln ['vɛksəln] *v.* : change **79**
Wecker (-) ['vɛkər] *n. m.* : alarm clock **12, 31**
Weg (e) [veːk] *n. m.* : track **61**
wehen ['veːən] *v.* : blow* **65**
Weihnachten (-) ['vaɪnaxtən] *n. nt.* :
  Christmas **90**
weiß [vaɪs] *adj.* : white **29**
weit [vaɪt] *adj.* : big **40**
werfen * ['vɛrfən] *v.* : throw* **87**
Wettbewerb (e) ['vɛtbə‚verp] *n. m.* :
  competition **79**
wetten ['vɛtən] *v.* : bet* **52**
Wetter (-) ['vɛtər] *n. nt.* : weather **67**

Wetterhahn (¨e) ['vɛtər‚haːn] *n. m.* :
  weathercock **68**
Wettkämpfer (-), **in** (nen) ['vɛt‚kɛmpfər] *n.* :
  athlete **84**
wiegen * ['viːgən] *v.* : weigh **20**
Wiese (n) ['viːzə] *n. f.* : meadow **62**
wild [vɪlt] *adj.* : wild **69**
Wimper (n) ['vɪmpər] *n. f.* : eyelash **48**
Wind (e) [vɪnt] *n. m.* : wind **65**
Winter (-) ['vɪntər] *n. m.* : winter **87**
wirklich ['vɪrklɪç] *adv.* : really **55, 77**
Wirkung (en) ['vɪrkʊŋ] *n. f.* : influence **26**
wissen * ['vɪsən] *v.* : know* **29, 41, 60**
Woche (n) ['vɔxə] *n. f.* : week **28**
wohnen ['voːnən] *v.* : live **9**
Wohnmobil (e) ['voːnmo‚biːl] *n. nt.* :
  camping car **74**
Wohnung (en) ['voːnʊŋ] *n. f.* : flat **93**
Wohnwagen (-) ['voːn‚vaːgən] *n. m.* : caravan **74**
Wohnzimmer (-) ['voːn‚tsɪmər] *n. nt.* :
  sitting-room **11, 69**; drawing room **93**
Wolke (n) ['vɔlkə] *n. f.* : cloud **66**
wollen * ['vɔlən] *v.* : want **20, 29, 53**

Y

Yoghurt (s) ['joːgʊrt] *n. m.* : yogurt **56**

Z

Zahl (en) [tsaːl] *n. f.* : figure **28**
zahlen ['tsaːlən] *v.* : pay* **21**
Zahn (¨e) [tsaːn] *n. m.* : tooth **15, 48**
Zahnbürste (n) ['tsaːn‚bʏrstə] *n. f.* :
  toothbrush **15**
Zahnpasta (en) ['tsaːn‚pasta] *n. f.* : toothpaste **15**
sich die Zähne putzen [zɪçdi'tsɛːnə‚pʊtsən] :
  brush one's teeth **15**
Zaun (¨e) [tsaʊn] *n. m.* : fence **62**
Zebra (s) ['tseːbra] *n. nt.* : zebra **69, 76**
Zebrastreifen (-) ['tseːbra‚ʃtraɪfən] *n. m.* :
  zebra crossing **23**
Zehe (n) ['tseːə] *n. f.* : toe **47**
zeigen ['tsaɪgən] *v.* : show* **31, 72**
den Weg zeigen [den've:k‚tsaɪgən] : show* the
  way **18**
Zeiger (-) ['tsaɪgər] *n. m.* : hand **31**
Zeit (en) [tsaɪt] *n. f.* : time **14**
Zelt (e) [tsɛlt] *n. nt.* : tent **74**
zelten ['tsɛltən] *v.* : camp **74**
Ziege (n) ['tsiːgə] *n. f.* : goat **62**
Ziel (n) [tsiːl] *n. nt.* : finish **84**
Zirkus (sse) ['tsɪrkʊs] *n. m.* : circus **93**
Zoll (¨e) [tsɔl] *n. m.* : customs *n. pl.* **72**
Zollbeamte(r), tin (nen) ['tsɔlbə‚ʔamtə] *n.* :
  customs officer **72**
Zoo (s) [tsoː] *n. m.* : zoo **76**
Zopf (¨e) [tsɔpf] *n. m.* : plait **37**
zornig ['tsɔrnɪç] *adj.* : angry **57**
zu [tsuː] *adv.* : too **40, 42, 62, 85**
Zucker (-) ['tsʊkər] *n. m.* : sugar **21, 55**
Zuckerdose (n) ['tsʊkər‚doːzə] *n. f.* :
  sugar dispenser **55**
zuerst [tsu'ʔerst] *adv.* : first of all **92**
zufrieden [tsu'friːdən] *adj.* : happy **38**
Zug (¨e) [tsuːk] *n. m.* : train **22**
zuhören ['tsu‚høːrən] *v.* : listen **30**
zumachen ['tsu‚maxən] *v.* : close* **84**
Zunge (n) ['tsʊŋə] *n. f.* : tongue **48**
zurückkommen * [tsu'rʏk‚kɔmən] *v.* :
  come* back **64**
Zuschauer (-), **in** (nen) ['tsu‚ʃaʊər] *n.* :
  spectator **93**; viewer **80**
zweite(r, s) ['tsvaɪtə] *adj.* : second **93**
Zwiebel (n) ['tsviːbəl] *n. f.* : onion **52**

English – German

A

actor, tress ['æktə^r, tris] *n.* : Schauspieler, in **80**
addition [ə'diʃ(ə)n] *n.* : Addieren *n. nt.* **28**
admire [əd'maiə^r] *v.* : bewundern **90**
(aero)plane [(ˈɛərə)plein] *n.* : Flugzeug *n. m.* **66, 72**
be*afraid [bi:ə'freid] : Angst haben* **10, 69**
air hostess [ɛə^rhoustis] *f.* : Stewardeß **72**
airport ['ɛəpɔ:t] *n.* : Flughafen *n. m.* **72**
aisle [aisl] *n.* : Gang *n. m.* **80**
alarm clock [ə'lɑ:mklɔk] : Wecker *n. m.* **12, 31**
a lot (of) [ə'lɔt(ɔv)] : viel **41, 56**
always ['ɔ:lwəz, -wiz] *adv.* : immer **29**
amazing [ə'meiziŋ] *adj.* : erstaunlich **69**
ambulance ['æmbjuləns] *n.* : Krankenwagen *n. m.* **49**
anchor ['æŋkə^r] *n.* : Anker *n. m.* **65**
angry ['æŋgri] *adj.* : zornig **57**
animal ['ænim(ə)l] *n.* : Tier *n. nt.* **68, 69, 76**
ankle boot ['æŋl(ə)lbu:t] : Halbstiefel *n. m.* **42**
anorak ['ænəræk] *n.* : Anorak *n. m.* **87**
ant [ænt] *n.* : Ameise *n. f.* **91**
appearance [ə'piərəns] *n.* : Aussehen *n. nt.* **36**
appearances [ə'piərənsiz] *n. pl.* : Schein *n. m.* **27**
apple ['æpl] *n.* : Apfel *n. m.* **53**
arithmetic [ə'riθmətik] *n.* : Rechnen *n. nt.* **28**
arm [ɑ:m] *n.* : Arm *n. m.* **35, 47**
armchair ['ɑmtʃɛə^r] *n.* : Sessel *n. m.* **11**
arrival [ə'raiv(ə)l] *n.* : Ankunft *n. f.* **72**
artist ['ɑ:tist] *n.* : Künstler, in **77**
ask for directions [ɑ:skfɔ:^rd(a)i'rekʃ(ə)ns] : nach dem Weg fragen **18**
at last [æt'lɑ:st] *adv.* : endlich **30, 62**
athlete ['æθli:t] *n.* : Wettkämpfer, in **84**
audience ['ɔ:djəns] *n.* : Publikum *n. nt.* **78**
aunt [ɑ:nt] *n. f.* : Tante **34**
autumn ['ɔ:təm] *n.* : Herbst *n. m.* **60**

B

baby ['beibi] *n.* : Baby *n. nt.* **35, 48**
babysitter ['beibisitə^r] *n.* : Babysitter *n. m.* **37**
back [bæk] *n.* : Rücken *n. m.* **46**; Hof *n. m.* **93**
baker ['beikə^r] *n.* : Bäcker, in **20**
bakery ['beikəri] *n.* : Bäckerei *n. f.* **20**
balcony ['bælkəni] *n.* : Balkon *n. m.* **9**
ball [bɔ:l] *n.* : Ball *n. m.* **75, 85, 86**; Kugel *n. f.* **90**
banana [bə'nɑ:nə] *n.* : Banane *n. f.* **53**
bank [bæŋk] *n.* : Ufer *n. m.* **64**
bank note ['bæŋknout] : Geldschein *n. m.* **21**
bannisters ['bænistəz] *n. pl.* : Geländer *n. m.* **10**
barometer [bə'rɔmitə^r] *n.* : Barometer *n. nt.* **67**
basket ['bɑ:skit] *n.* : Korb *n. m.* **91**
bat [bæt] *n.* : Schläger *n. m.* **86**
bath [bɑ:θ] *n.* : Badewanne *n. f.* **15**
have*a bath [[hævə'bɑ:θ] : baden **15**
bathing suit [beiθiŋs(j)u:t] : Badeanzug *n. m.* **73**
bathrobe ['bɑ:θroub] *n.* : Bademantel *n. m.* **15**
bathroom ['bɑ:θru:m] *n.* : Badezimmer *n. nt.* **15**

be*[bi:] *v.* : sein* **21, 35, 85**
beach [bi:tʃ] *n.* : Strand *n. m.* **73**
beach umbrella [bi:tʃʌm'brelə] : Sonnenschirm *n. m.* **73**
bead [bi:d] *n.* : Perle *n. f.* **43**
bear ['bɛə^r] *n.* : Bär *n. m.* **30, 38**
beard [biəd] *n.* : Bart *n. m.* **37**
beautiful ['bju:tif(u)l] *adj.* : schön **62, 93**
bed [bed] *n.* : Bett *n. nt.* **13**
bedroom ['bedru(:)m] *n.* : Schlafzimmer *n. nt.* **12**
bedside table ['bedsaidteibl] : Nachttisch *n. m.* **12**
bee [bi:] *n.* : Biene *n. f.* **63**
believe [bi'li:v] *v.* : glauben **9**
belt [belt] *n.* : Gürtel *n. m.* **41**
bench [ben(t)ʃ] *n.* : Bank *n. f.* **81**
best [best] *adj.* : beste(r, s) **29**
bet* [bet] *v.* : wetten **52**
better ['betə^r] *adv.* : besser **72**
bicycle ['baisikl] *n.* : Fahrrad *n. nt.* **18**
big [big] *adj.* : weit **40**; groß *adj.* **42**
bike [baik] *n.* : Fahrrad *n. nt.* **19**
bird [bɜ:d] *n.* : Vogel *n. m.* **61, 62**
birthday ['bə:θdei] *n.* : Geburtstag *n. m.* **92**
birthday party ['bə:θdei'pɑ:ti] : Geburtstagsfeier *n. f.* **92**
black [blæk] *adj.* : schwarz **29**
blackboard ['blækbɔ:d] *n.* : Tafel *n. f.* **26**
blanket ['blæŋkit] *n.* : Decke *n. f.* **12**
blond, blonde [blɔnd] *adj.* : blond **37**
blouse [blauz] *n.* : Bluse *n. f.* **39**
blow* [blou] *v.* : blasen* **92**; wehen **65**
blue [blu:] *adj.* : blau **29**
boat [bout] *n.* : Boot *n. nt.* **65**
body ['bɔdi] *n.* : Körper *n. m.* **46, 47**
bone [boun] *n.* : Knochen *n. m.* **54**
book [buk] *n.* : Buch *n. nt.* **11, 27, 30**
boot [bu:t] *n.* : Stiefel *n. m.* **42**
bottle [bɔtl] *n.* : Flasche *n. f.* **56**
bottom ['bɔtəm] *n.* : Hintern *n. m.* **46**
bouquet [bu'kei] *n.* : Strauß *n. m.* **63**
bow tie [boutai] : Fliege *n. f.* **39**
boy [bɔi] *n. m.* : Junge **35**
bracelet ['breislit] *n.* : Armband *n. nt.* **43**
branch [brɑ:n(t)ʃ] *n.* : Ast *n. m.* **60**
bread [bred] *n.* : Brot *n. m.* **55**
break* [breik] *v.* : kaputtmachen **14**
breakfast ['brekfəst] *n.* : Frühstück *n. nt.* **55**
breast [brest] *n.* : Flügel *n. m.* **90**
breathe [bri:θ] *v.* : atmen **49**
bridge [bridʒ] *n.* : Brücke *n. f.* **64**
brooch [broutʃ] *n.* : Brosche *n. f.* **43**
brook [bruk] *n.* : Bach *n. m.* **62**
brown [braun] *adj.* : braun **29**
brush one's teeth [brʌʃwʌnsti:θ] : sich die Zähne putzen **15**
build* [bild] *v.* : bauen **64**
building ['bildiŋ] *n.* : Gebäude *n. nt.* **18**
building block ['bildiŋblɔk] : Bauklotz *n. m.* **75**
bullfighter [bulfaitə^r] *n.* : Torero *n. m.* **40**
bus [bʌs] *n.* : Bus *n. m.* **23**
bus fare [bʌsfɛə^r] : Busfahrschein *n. m.* **28**
bus stop [bʌsstɔp] : Bushaltestelle *n. f.* **23**
butcher ['bʌtʃə^r] *n.* : Fleischer *n. m.* **20**

butcher's shop ['bʌtʃəsʃɔp] : Fleischerei *n. f.* **20**
butter ['bʌtə^r] *n.* : Butter *n. f.* **55**
butterfly ['bʌtəflai] *n.* : Schmetterling *n. m.* **85**
butterfly net ['bʌtəflainet] : Schmetterlingsnetz *n. nt.* **85**
buy* [bai] *v.* : kaufen **9, 21, 52**
bye! [bai] *interj.* : auf Wiedersehen! **8, 14**

C

cabbage ['kæbidʒ] *n.* : Kohl *n. m.* **52**
cage [keidʒ] *n.* : Käfig *n. f.* **93**
cake [keik] *n.* : Kuchen *n. m.* **14, 92**
calf *pl.* **calves** [kɑ:f, kɑ:vz] *n.* : Kalb *n. nt.* **62**
camel ['kæm(ə)l] *n.* : Kamel *n. nt.* **76**
camera ['kæm(ə)rə] *n.* : Fotoapparat *n. m.* **91**
camp [kæmp] *v.* : zelten **74**
camping ['kæmpiŋ] *n.* : Campingplatz *n. m.* **74**
camping car ['kæmpiŋkɑ:^r] : Wohnmobil *n. nt.* **74**
can* [kæn] *v.* : können* **80**
candle ['kænd(ə)l] *n.* : Kerze *n. f.* **92**
canoe [kə'nu:] *n.* : Kanu *n. nt.* **64**
canvas ['kænvəs] *n.* : Leinwand *n. f.* **77**
cap [kæp] *n.* : Mütze *n. f.* **41**; Schirmmütze *n. f.* **40**
car [kɑ:^r] *n.* : Wagen *n. m.* **18, 19**
caravan ['kærəvæn] *n.* : Wohnwagen *n. m.* **74**
carnation [kɑ:'neiʃ(ə)n] *n.* : Nelke *n. f.* **63**
car park [kɑ:^rpɑ:k] : Parkplatz *n. m.* **18**
carriage ['kæridʒ] *n.* : Wagen **22**
carrot ['kærət] *n.* : Karotte *n. f.* **52**
cashier [kæ'ʃiə^r] *n.* : Kassierer, in **21**
cash register [kæʃ'redʒistə^r] : Kasse *n. f.* **21**
cat [kæt] *n.* : Katze *n. f.* **68**
catch* [kætʃ] *v.* : fangen* **76**; angeln **64**
cause [kɔ:z] *v.* : verursachen **19**
century ['sentjuri] *n.* : Jahrhundert *n. nt.* **93**
cereal ['siəriəl] *n.* : Müsli *n. nt.* **55**
chair [tʃɛə^r] *n.* : Stuhl *n. m.* **54**
chalet ['ʃælei] *n.* : Hütte *n. f.* **61**
chamois ['ʃæmwɑ:] *n.* : Gemse *n. f.* **61**
champion ['tʃæmpiən] *n.* : Champion **84**
change [tʃein(d)ʒ] *v.* : wechseln **79**
change [tʃein(d)ʒ] *n.* : Wechselgeld *n. nt.* **21**
cheap [tʃi:p] *adj.* : billig **21**
checkers ['tʃekəz] *n. pl.* : Damespiel *n. nt.* **75**
cheek [tʃi:k] *n.* : Wange *n. f.* **48**
cheese [tʃi:z] *n.* : Käse *n. m.* **56**
cherry ['tʃeri] *n.* : Kirsche *n. f.* **53**
chess [tʃes] *n.* : Schachspiel *n. nt.* **75**
chestnut ['tʃes(t)nʌt] *n.* : Kastanie *n. f.* **60**
chicken ['tʃikin] *n.* : Hähnchen *n. nt.* **20, 56, 91**
chief [tʃi:f] *n.* : Häuptling *n. m.* **38**
child *pl.* **children** [tʃaild, 'tʃildrən] *n.* : Kind *n. nt.* **27, 35**
chimney ['tʃimni] *n.* : Schornstein *n. m.* **9**
chin [tʃin] *n.* : Kinn *n. nt.* **48**
chocolate ['tʃɔklət] *n.* : Schokolade *n. f.* **92**
choose* [tʃu:z] *v.* : aussuchen **69**
Christmas ['krisməs] *n.* : Weihnachten *n. nt.* **90**

cinema ['sinəmə] n. : Kino n. nt. **80**
circle ['sə:k(ə)l] n. : Kreis n. m. **30**
circus ['sə:kəs] n. : Zirkus n. m. **93**
clap [klæp] v. : applaudieren **78**
class [klɑs] n. : Klasse n. f. **26**
classroom ['klɑːsruːm] n. : Klassenzimmer
  n. nt. **26**
clean [kliːn] adj. : reinlich **15**
clean up [kliːnʌp] v. : putzen **34**
clearing [kliəriŋ] n. : Lichtung n. f. **60**
clock [klɔk] n. : Uhr n. f. **22**
close* [klouz] v. : zumachen **84**
clothes [klouðz] n. pl. : Kleidung n. f. **39, 40, 41**
cloud [klaud] n. : Wolke n. f. **66**
clown [klaun] n. : Clown n. m. **93**
coat [kout] n. : Mantel n. m. **40**
coatstand [kout'stænd] n. : Kleiderständer
  n. m. **40**
cock [kɔk] n. : Hahn n. m. **68**
coffee ['kɔfi] n. : Kaffee n. m. **55**
coffee-pot ['kɔfipɔt] n. : Kaffeekanne n. f. **55**
coin [kɔin] n. : Geldstück n. nt. **21**
cold [kould] adj. : kalt **74, 87, 91**
colour ['kʌlər] n. : Farbe n. f. **29**
comb [koum] n. : Kamm n. m. **15**
come* back [kʌmbæk] v. : zurückkommen* **64**
comfortable ['kʌmfətəbl] adj. : bequem **11**
competition [kɔmpi'tiʃ(ə)n] n. : Wettbewerb
  n. m. **79**
concentrate [kɔnsəntreit] v. : konzentrieren **84**
concert ['kɔnsət] n. : Konzert n. nt. **78, 79**
conductor [kən'dʌktər] n. : Dirigent n. m. **78**
cook [kuk] v. : kochen **14**
cooker ['kukər] n. : Herd n. m. **14**
counter ['kauntər] n. : Theke n. f. **21**
country(side) ['kʌntri(said)] n. : Land n. nt. **62**
court shoe [kɔːtʃuː] : Pumps n. m. **42**
cousin ['kʌz(ə)n] n. m. : Vetter **34, 36**
cow [kau] n. : Kuh n. f. **68**
cream [kriːm] n. : Sahne n. f. **14**
crocodile ['krɔkədail] n. : Krokodil n. nt. **69**
crossroads ['krɔsrouds] n. pl. : Kreuzung n. f. **18**
cross (the street) [krɔs(θəstriːt)] v. : über die
  Straße gehen* **19**
cuckoo clock ['kukuːklɔk] : Kuckucksuhr n. f. **31**
cup [kʌp] n. : Tasse n. f. **55**
cupboard ['kʌbəd] n. : Küchenschrank n. m. **14**
customs ['kʌstəms] n. pl. : Zoll n. m. **72**
customs officer ['kʌstəms'ɔfisər] :
  Zollbeamte(r), tin **72**
cut* [kʌt] v. : schneiden* **35**
cute [kjuːt] adj. : niedlich **48**

D

daisy ['deizi] n. : Margerite n. f. **63**
dance [dɑːns] v. : tanzen **79**
dance [dɑːns] n. : Ball n. m. **39**
dangerous ['dein(d)ʒ(ə)rəs] adj. : gefährlich
  62, 85
dark [dɑːk] adj. : dunkel **10, 29**; braunhaarig **37**
daughter ['dɔːtər] n. f. : Tochter **34**
day [dei] n. : Tag n. m. **68**
decide [di'said] v. : beschließen* **68**
deep [diːp] adj. : tief **64**
deer ['diər] n. inv. : Reh n. nt. **61**
delicious [di'liʃəs] adj. : lecker **56, 60**
departure [di'pɑːtjər] n. : Abflug n. m. **72**
desk [desk] n. : Schreibtisch n. m. **26**
die* [dai] v. : sterben* **49**
dinner ['dinər] n. : Abendessen n. nt. **57**
diploma [di'ploumə] n. : Diplom n. nt. **47**
direction [d(a)i'rekʃ(ə)n] n. : Richtung n. f. **23**
dirty ['də:ti] adj. : schmutzig **15**
dish [diʃ] n. : Platte n. f. **54, 56**
do* the dishes [duːθədiʃiz] : das Geschirr
  spülen **14**

division [di'viʒ(ə)n] n. : Dividieren n. nt. **28**
doctor ['dɔktər] n. : Arzt n. m. **49**
dog [dɔg] n. : Hund, Hündin **68**
doll [dɔl] n. : Puppe n. f. **9, 75**
dollar ['dɔlər] n. : Dollar n. m. **28, 47**
domino ['dɔminou] n. : Dominostein n. nt. **75**
door [dɔːr] n. : Tür n. f. **9**
do* the dishes [duːθədiʃiz] : das Geschirr
  spülen **14**
draught-board [drɑːftbɔːd] n. : Damebrett
  n. nt. **75**
drawer ['drɔːər] n. : Schublade n. f. **41**
drawing room ['drɔːiŋruːm] : Wohnzimmer **93**
dress [dres] n. : Kleid n. nt. **39**
dressing gown ['dresiŋgaun] : Morgenmantel
  n. m. **13**
drink* [driŋk] v. : trinken* **55**
drive* [draiv] v. : fahren* **23, 62**
drive* mad [draivmæd] : auf die Nerven
  gehen* **11**
driver ['draivər] n. : Fahrer, in **23**
drums [drʌms] n. pl. : Schlagzeug n. nt. **79**
duck [dʌk] n. : Ente n. f. **68**
dustbin ['dʌs(t)bin] n. : Mülleimer n. m. **14**
dynamite ['dainəmait] n. : Sprengstoff n. m. **19**

E

eagle ['iːgl] n. : Adler n. m. **60, 61**
early ['ə:li] adv. : früh **62**
ear ['iər] n. : Ohr n. nt. **48**
earring ['iːəriŋ] n. : Ohrring n. m. **43**
eat* [iːt] v. : essen* **54, 56, 60, 77, 92**
egg [eg] n. : Ei n. nt. **55, 60, 61**
eiderdown ['aidədaun] n. : Federbett n. nt. **13**
elbow ['elbou] n. : Ellenbogen n. m. **47**
electric [i'lektrik] adj. : elektrisch **79**
elephant ['elifənt] n. : Elefant n. m. **69**
emerald ['em(ə)rəld] n. : Smaragd n. m. **43**
empty ['em(p)ti] adj. : leer **30**
end [end] n. : Ende n. nt. **84**
engine ['endʒin] n. : Lokomotive n. f. **22**
enthrall [in'θrɔːl] v. : fesseln **80**
excellent ['eksələnt] adj. : ausgezeichnet **26**
exercise book ['eksəsaizbuk] : Heft n. nt. **28**
expensive [eks'pensiv] adj. : teuer **21, 77**
explain [eks'plein] v. : erklären **63**
explanation [eksplə'neiʃ(ə)n] n. : Erklärung
  n. f. **65**
eye [ai] n. : Auge n. nt. **48, 84**
eyebrow ['aibrau] n. : Augenbraue n. f. **48**
eyelash ['ailæʃ] n. : Wimper n. f. **48**

F

face [feis] n. : Gesicht n. nt. **48**
faithful ['feiθf(u)l] adj. : treu **68**
fall* [fɔːl] v. : fallen* **60, 87**
fall* asleep [fɔːlə'sliːp] v. : einschlafen* **62**
family ['fæm(i)li] n. : Familie n. f. **34**
famous ['feiməs] adj. : berühmt **38**
farm [fɑːm] n. : Bauernhof n. m. **68**
farmer ['fɑːmər] n. : Bauer, Bäuerin **68**
fat [fæt] adj. : dick **36**
father ['fɑːðər] n. m. : Vater **34**
fence [fens] n. : Zaun n. m. **62**
fertilizer ['fə:tilaizər] n. : Dünger n. m. **62**
fight* back [faitbæk] v. : sich verteidigen **80**
figure ['figər] n. : Zahl n. f. **28**
film [film] n. : Film n. m. **80**
find* [faind] v. : finden* **39, 60, 61**
finger ['fiŋgər] n. : Finger n. m. **47**
finish ['finiʃ] n. : Ziel n. nt. **84**

fireplace ['faiəpleis] n. : Kamin n. m. **90**
fire ['faiər] n. : Feuer n. nt. **74**
fir tree [fə:'triː] : Tanne n. f. **64**
first [fə:st] adj. : erste(r, s) **40, 93**
first of all [fə:stɔvɔːl] adv. : zuerst **92**
fish bowl [fiʃboul] : Aquarium n. nt. **11**
fish pl. **fishes** [fiʃ, 'fiʃiz] n. : Fisch **57, 64, 76**
fisherman pl. **-men** ['fiʃəmæn, -men] n. m. :
  Angler **64**
fishing rod ['fiʃiŋrɔd] : Angel n. f. **64**
flat [flæt] n. : Wohnung n. f. **93**
floor [flɔːr] n. : Boden n. m. **43**; Fußboden
  n. m. **10**; Stock n. m. **93**
flow [flou] v. : fließen* **64**
flower ['flauər] n. : Blume n. f. **8, 63**
flute [fluːt] n. : Flöte n. f. **78**
fly* [flai] v. : fliegen* **62**
flying saucer [flain'sɔːsər] :
  fliegende Untertasse f. **66**
fog [fɔg] n. : Nebel n. m. **62**
food [fuːd] n. : Nahrung n. f. **51**
foot pl. **feet** [fut, fiːt] n. : Fuß **42, 47**
forehead ['fɔrid, 'fɔːhed] n. : Stirn n. f. **48**
forest ['fɔrist] n. : Wald n. m. **60**
forget* [fə'get] v. : vergessen* **22, 41, 84**
fork [fɔːk] n. : Gabel n. f. **54**
fountain ['fauntin] n. : Brunnen n. m. **81**
fridge [fridʒ] n. : Kühlschrank n. m. **57**
friend [frend] n. : Freund, in **27**
fringe [frindʒ] n. : Pony n. m. **37**
frown [fraun] v. : die Stirn runzeln **46**
fruit [fruːt] n. : Frucht n. f. **53**; Obst n. nt. **53**
frying pan ['fraiŋpæn] : Pfanne n. f. **57**
full [ful] adj. : voll **30**
have* fun [hævfʌn] : Spaß haben* **27, 75**;
  amüsieren **42**

G

game [geim] n. : Spiel n. nt. **75, 86**; Partie n. f. **75**
garage ['gærɑːʒ] n. : Garage n. f. **9**
garden ['gɑːd(ə)n] n. : Garten n. m. **8, 69**
garland ['gɑːlənd] n. : Girlande n. f. **90**
gentleman pl. **-men** ['dʒent(ə)lmæn, -men] n. m. :
  Herr **23**
get* changed [get'tʃein(d)ʒd] : umziehen* **92**
get* dressed [get'dresd] v. : sich anziehen* **40**
get* up [getʌp] v. : aufstehen* **12**
giraffe [dʒi'ræf, -'rɑːf] n. : Giraffe n. f. **69, 76**
girl [gə:l] n. f. : Mädchen n. nt. **23, 35, 37, 39**
give* [giv] v. : geben* **92**
glad [glæd] adj. : froh **74**
glass [glɑːs] n. : Glas n. nt. **14, 54**
glasses [glɑːsiz] n. pl. : Brille n. f. **46**
glitter ['glitər] v. : glänzen **43**
globe [gloub] n. : Erdkugel n. f. **30**
go* [gou] v. : gehen* **20, 39, 57, 76**
goat [gout] n. : Ziege n. f. **62**
gold [gould] n. : Gold n. nt. **43**
goldfish ['gouldfiʃ] n. : Goldfisch n. m. **11**
good [gud] adj. : gut **29, 79**
go* to bed [goutuːbed] : schlafen gehen* **75**
grandfather ['græn(d)fɑːðər] n. m. : Großvater **34**
grandmother ['græn(d)mʌðər] n. f. :
  Großmutter **34**
grape [greip] n. : Traube n. f. **53**
grass [grɑːs] n. : Gras n. nt. **60**
green [griːn] adj. : grün **18, 29**
green bean [griːnbiːn] : grüne Bohne n. f. **52**
grey [grei] adj. : grau **29**
grill [gril] v. : grillen **74**
grocer's shop ['grousəzʃɔp] :
  Lebensmittelgeschäft n. nt. **20**
grow* [grou] v. : wachsen* **52**
guard [gɑːd] v. : bewachen **68**
guest [gest] n. : Gast n. m. **40, 92**
guitar [gi'tɑːr] n. : Gitarre n. f. **74, 79**

gym [dʒim] *n.* : Sporthalle *n. f.* **85**
gymnastics [dʒim'næstiks] *n. pl.* : Gymnastik *n. f.* **85**

H

hair ['hɛəʳ] *n.* : Haar *n. nt.* **35, 37, 48**
half an hour ['hɑːfən'auəʳ] : halbe Stunde *f.* **35**
hall [hɔːl] *n.* : Flur *n. m.* **10**
hand [hænd] *n.* : Hand *n. f.* **47**; Zeiger *n. m.* **31**
hand basin [hænd'beis(ə)n] : Waschbecken *n. nt.* **15**
hangar ['hæŋəʳ] *n.* : Flugzeughalle *n. f.* **72**
hang* up [hæŋʌp] *v.* : hängen* **67**
happen ['hæp(ə)n] *v.* : los sein* **76**
happy ['hæpi] *adj.* : froh **30, 31**; fröhlich **15**; glücklich **35**; zufrieden **38**
harbour ['hɑːbəʳ] *n.* : Hafen *n. m.* **65**
harp [hɑːp] *n.* : Harfe *n. f.* **79**
hat [hæt] *n.* : Hut *n. m.* **40, 80**
head [hed] *n.* : Kopf *n. m.* **46**
have* a **headache** [hævə'hedeik] : Kopfschmerzen haben* **49**
headlight ['hedlait] *n.* : Scheinwerfer *n. m.* **19**
headmaster [hed'mɑːstəʳ] *n.* : Direktor, in **26**
health [helθ] *n.* : Gesundheit *n. f.* **49**
heart [hɑːt] *n.* : Herz *n. nt.* **49**
heavy ['hevi] *adj.* : schwer **22**
hectic ['hektik] *adj.* : unruhig **66**
hedge [hedʒ] *n.* : Hecke *n. f.* **8**
heel [hiːl] *n.* : Absatz *n. m.* **42**
help [help] *v.* : helfen* **28, 87**
help [help] *n.* : Hilfe *n. f.* **26**
help! [help] *interj.* : Hilfe! **72**
hen [hen] *n.* : Huhn *n. nt.* **68**
henhouse ['henhaus] *n.* : Hühnerstall *n. m.* **68**
hero ['hiərou, -rouz] *n.* : Held *n. m.* **80**
hide* [haid] *v.* : sich verstecken **76**
hippopotamus *pl.* **-muses, -mi** [hipə'pɔtəməs, -məsiz, -mai] *n.* : Nilpferd *n. nt.* **69**
hold* [hould] *v.* : halten* **35**
holiday ['hɔlidei] *n.* : Fest *n. nt.* **89**
holidays ['hɔlideiz] *n. pl.* : Ferien *n. pl.* **22**; Urlaub *n. m.* **73**
homework ['houmwərk] *n.* : Hausaufgaben *n. f. pl.* **28**
honey ['hʌni] *n.* : Honig *n. m.* **55**
hoot [huːt] *v.* : hupen **19**
hope [houp] *v.* : hoffen **29**
horse [hɔːs] *n.* : Pferd *n. nt.* **68**
hospital ['hɔspit(ə)l] *n.* : Krankenhaus *n. nt.* **49**
hour ['auəʳ] *n.* : Stunde *n. f.* **31, 35**
house [haus] *n.* : Haus *n. nt.* **7, 9, 10, 67, 68**
human ['hjuːm(ə)n] *adj.* : menschlich *adj.* **45**
be* **hungry** [biː'hʌŋgri] : hungrig sein* **54**
hunt [hʌnt] *v.* : jagen **38**
hurry ['hʌri] *v.* : sich beeilen **93**
husband ['hʌzbənd] *n. m.* : Mann **34**

I

ice cream ['aiskriːm] : Eis *n. nt.* **92**
idea [ai'diːə] *n.* : Idee *n. f.* **66, 68**
impossible [im'pɔsibl] *adj.* : unmöglich **9**
Indian ['indiən] *n.* : Indianer, in **38, 64**
influence ['influəns] *n.* : Wirkung *n. f.* **26**
injection [in'dʒekʃ(ə)n] *n.* : Spritze *n. f.* **49**
inkwell ['iŋkwel] *n.* : Tintenfaß *n. nt.* **30**
instrument ['instrumənt] *n.* : Instrument *n. nt.* **79**
invitation [invi'teiʃ(ə)n] *n.* : Einladung *n. f.* **92**
invite [in'vait] *v.* : einladen **38**

J

jacket ['dʒækit] *n.* : Jacke *n. f.* **39**; Jackett *n. nt.* **40**
jam [dʒæm] *n.* : Marmelade *n. f.* **55**
jeans [dʒiːnz] *n. pl.* : Jeans *n. pl.* **40**
jetty ['dʒeti] *n.* : Mole *n. f.* **65**
jewellery ['dʒuːəlri] *n.* : Schmuck *n. m.* **43**
job [dʒɔb] *n.* : Arbeit *n. f.* **29**
juggler ['dʒʌgləʳ] *n.* : Jongleur *n. m.* **93**
juice [dʒuːs] *n.* : Saft *n. m.* **92**
jump [dʒʌmp] *v.* : springen* **76, 84**

K

kangaroo [kæŋgə'ruː] *n.* : Känguruh *n. nt.* **76**
keep* one's mouth shut [kiːpwʌnsmauθʃʌt] : schweigen* **38**
kennel ['ken(ə)l] *n.* : Hundehütte *n. f.* **68**
key [kiː] *n.* : Schlüssel *n. m.* **9**
kilo ['kiːlou] *n.* : Kilo *n. nt.* **20**
kitchen ['kitʃin] *n.* : Küche *n. f.* **14, 57**
kite [kait] *n.* : Drachen *n. m.* **66, 91**
knee [niː] *n.* : Knie *n. nt.* **47**
knife *pl.* **knives** [naif, naivz] *n.* : Messer *n. nt.* **54**
know* [nou] *v.* : wissen* **29, 41, 60**

L

ladle ['leidl] *n.* : Suppenkelle *n. f.* **57**
lady ['leidi] *n. f.* : Dame **23, 46**
lamp [læmp] *n.* : Lampe *n. f.* **12**
land [lænd] *v.* : landen **72**
landscape ['læn(d)skeip] *n.* : Landschaft *n. f.* **62**
late [leit] *adv.* : spät **13, 29**
be* **late** [biː'leit] : sich verspäten **22**
lawn [lɔːn] *n.* : Rasen *n. m.* **8**
lawn mower ['lɔːnmouəʳ] : Rasenmäher *n. m.* **8**
leaf *pl.* **leaves** [liːf, liːvz] *n.* : Blatt *n. nt.* **60**
learn* [lən] *v.* : lernen **27**; beibringen* **30**
leave* [liːv] *v.* : lassen* **54**
leek [liːk] *n.* : Lauch *n. m.* **52**
leg [leg] *n.* : Bein *n. nt.* **47**; Keule *n. f.* **56, 90**
leisure ['leʒəʳ] *n.* : Freizeit *n. f.* **71**
lemonade [lemə'neid] *n.* : Limonade *n. f.* **92**
let* [let] *v.* : lassen* **13**
lettuce ['letis] *n.* : Salat *n. m.* **52**
light [lait] *adj.* : hell **29**
light [lait] *n.* : Licht *n. nt.* **10**
lighthouse ['laithaus] *n.* : Leuchtturm *n. m.* **65**
lightning ['laitniŋ] *n.* : Blitz *n. m.* **67**
like [laik] *v.* : mögen* **57**
lion ['laiən] *n.* : Löwe, in **69**
listen ['lis(ə)n] *v.* : zuhören **30**
live [liv] *v.* : wohnen **9**
lock [lɔk] *n.* : Schloß *n. nt.* **9**
log [lɔg] *n.* : Holzscheit *n. nt.* **90**
lollipop ['lɔlipɔp] *n.* : Lutscher *n. m.* **92**
long [lɔŋ] *adj.* : lang **37, 69**
look after [luk'ɑːftəʳ] *v.* : pflegen **49**
look for [lukfɔːʳ] *v.* : suchen **93**
lorry ['lɔri] *n.* : Lastwagen *n. m.* **23**
love [lʌv] *v.* : lieben **8**
lovely ['lʌvli] *adj.* : schön **9, 31, 39, 53**
luck [lʌk] *n.* : Glück *n. nt.* **31**
luggage ['lʌgidʒ] *n.* : Gepäck *n. nt.* **22**
lunch [lʌn(t)ʃ] *n.* : Mittagessen *n. nt.* **56**
be* **lying down** [biːlaiŋdaun] : liegen* **47**

M

man *pl.* **men** [mæn, men] *n. m.* : Mann **35**
marble ['mɑːbl] *n.* : Murmel *n. f.* **27**
masseur, euse [mæ'səʳ, mæ'səːz] *n.* : Masseur, in **47**
masterpiece ['mɑːstəpiːs] *n.* : Meisterwerk *n. nt.* **77**
mattress ['mætris] *n.* : Matratze *n. f.* **12**
meadow ['medou] *n.* : Wiese *n. f.* **62**
meal [miːl] *n.* : Essen *n. nt.* **91**
meat [miːt] *n.* : Fleisch *n. nt.* **56, 74**
medal ['med(ə)l] *n.* : Medaille *n. f.* **84**
medicine ['med(i)sin] *n.* : Medizin *n. f.* **14, 49**
mess [mes] *n.* : Durcheinander *n. nt.* **34**
microphone ['maikrəfoun] *n.* : Mikro *n. nt.* **79**
milk [milk] *n.* : Milch *n. f.* **21, 55**
minute ['minit] *n.* : Minute *n. f.* **31**
mirror ['mirəʳ] *n.* : Spiegel *n. m.* **15**
make* a **mistake** [meikəmis'teik] : sich verrechnen **28**
mobile ['moubail] *n.* : Mobile *n. nt.* **75**
money ['mʌni] *n.* : Geld *n. nt.* **21**
monkey ['mʌŋki] *n.* : Affe *n. m.* **69**
month [mɔnθ] *n.* : Monat *n. m.* **93**
moon [muːn] *n.* : Mond *n. m.* **66**
morning ['mɔːniŋ] *n.* : Morgen *n. m.* **52, 62**
moth [mɔθ] *n.* : Motte *n. f.* **41**
mother ['mʌðəʳ] *n. f.* : Mutter **34, 35**
motorcycle ['moutəsaikl] *n.* : Motorrad *n. nt.* **23**
mountain ['mauntin] *n.* : Gebirge *n. nt.* **61**
mountain stream ['mauntinstriːm] : Gebirgsbach *n. m.* **61**
moustache [məs'tɑːʃ] *n.* : Schnurrbart *n. m.* **37**
mouth [mauθ] *n.* : Mund *n. m.* **48**
multiplication [mʌltipli'keiʃ(ə)n] *n.* : Multiplizieren *n. nt.* **28**
muscled ['mʌsld] *adj.* : muskulös **47**
museum [mju(ː)'ziəm] *n.* : Museum *n. nt.* **61**
mushroom ['mʌʃrum] *n.* : Pilz *n. m.* **60**
music ['mjuːzik] *n.* : Musik *n. f.* **78, 79**
musician [mju'ziʃ(ə)n] *n.* : Musiker, in **79**

N

napkin ['næpkin] *n.* : Serviette *n. f.* **54**
narrow ['nærou] *adj.* : schmal **10**
nature ['neitjəʳ] *n.* : Natur *n. f.* **59**
neck [nek] *n.* : Hals *n. m.* **46, 69**
necklace ['neklis] *n.* : Halskette *n. f.* **43**
need [niːd] *v.* : brauchen **36**
nephew Neffe *n. m.* **55**
nephew ['nefju] *n. m.* : Neffe **92**
nest [nest] *n.* : Nest *n. nt.* **60**
net [net] *n.* : Netz *n. nt.* **86**
new [njuː] *adj.* : neu **39, 69**
nice [nais] *adj.* : nett **38**
niece [niːs] *n. f.* : Nichte *n. f.* **37**
night [nait] *n.* : Nacht *n. f.* **66**
nightcap ['naitkæp] *n.* : Nachtmütze *n. f.* **13**
now [nau] *adv.* : jetzt **66, 72, 92**
nurse [nəːs] *n.* : Krankenschwester *n. f.* **49**

O

okay! ['ou'kei] *interj.* : einverstanden! **92**
old [ould] *adj.* : alt **36**
omelet ['ɔmlit] *n.* : Omelett *n. nt.* **60**
onion ['ʌnjən] *n.* : Zwiebel *n. f.* **52**
open ['oup(ə)n] *v.* : aufmachen **84**
orange ['ɔrin(d)ʒ] *n.* : Orange *n. f.* **53, 92**
orange ['ɔrin(d)ʒ] *adj.* : orange **29**

orange squeezer ['ɔrin(d)ʒ'skwi:zəʳ] : Entsafter n. m. 36
orchestra ['ɔ:kistrə] n. : Orchester n. nt. 78
ostrich ['ɔ'striʃ] n. : Strauß n. m. 76
other ['ʌθəʳ] adj. : andere(r, s) 76
be* **out of work** [bi:autɔv'wə:k] : arbeitslos sein* 36
oven ['ʌv(ə)n] n. : Ofen n. m. 14
owl [aul] n. : Eule n. f. 66

P

page [peidʒ] n. : Seite n. f. 26
paint [peint] v. : malen 77
paint brush [peint'brʌʃ] : Pinsel n. m. 77
painting ['peintiŋ] n. : Bild n. nt. 77; Gemälde n. nt. 77, 93
palette ['pælit] n. : Palette n. f. 77
palm tree [pɑ:mtri:] : Palme n. f. 73
paper [peipəʳ] n. : Papier n. nt. 77
paper ['peipəʳ] v. : tapezieren 69
parade [pə'reid] v. : vorbeiziehen* 93
parcel ['pɑ:s(ə)l] n. : Paket n. nt. 19
park [pɑ:k] n. : Park n. m. 81
park [pɑ:k] v. : parken 18
part [pɑ:t] n. : Teil n. m. 47
passenger ['pæsəndʒəʳ] n. : Fahrgast n. m. 23
passport ['pɑ:spɔ:t] n. : Paß n. m. 72
path [pɑ:θ] n. : Gartenweg n. m. 8
pavement ['peivmənt] n. : Bürgersteig n. m. 18
pay* [pei] v. : zahlen 21
pea [pi:] n. : Erbse n. f. 52
peach [pi:tʃ] n. : Pfirsich n. m. 53
peak [pi:k] n. : Gipfel n. m. 61
pear ['pɛəʳ] n. : Birne n. f. 53
pebble [pebl] n. : Kieselstein n. m. 64
pedestrian [pi'destriən] n. : Fußgänger, in 19
peg [peg] n. : Kleiderständer n. m. 41
pen [pen] n. : Kugelschreiber n. m. 28
pencil ['pens(ə)l] n. : Bleistift n. m. 77
penguin ['peŋgwin] n. : Pinguin n. m. 76
people ['pi:pl] n. : Leute n. pl. 33
pepper ['pepəʳ] n. : Pfeffer n. m. 54
performance [pə'fɔ:məns] n. : Vorstellung n. f. 93
performer [pə'fɔ:məʳ] n. : Artist n. m. 93
perhaps [pə'hæps, præps] adv. : vielleicht 49
personality [pə:sə'næliti] n. : Persönlichkeit n. f. 38
petal [pet(ə)l] n. : Blütenblatt n. nt. 63
petticoat ['petikout] n. : Unterrock n. m. 39
photo ['foutou] n. : Foto n. nt. 46, 91
take* a **photo** [teikə'foutou] : ein Foto machen 46, 91
piano [pi'ænou] n. : Klavier n. nt. 78
pick up ['pikʌp] v. : abholen 37
picnic ['piknik] n. : Picknick n. nt. 91
pig [pig] n. : Schwein n. nt. 62, 68
pillow [pilou] n. : Kopfkissen n. nt. 13
pineapple ['painæpl] n. : Ananas n. f. 53
pink [piŋk] adj. : rosa adj. inv. 29
plait [plæt] n. : Zopf n. m. 37
plant [plɑ:nt] n. : Pflanze n. f. 52, 63
plant [plɑ:nt] v. : pflanzen 8
plate [pleit] n. : Teller n. m. 14, 54
platform ['plætfɔ:m] n. : Bahnsteig n. m. 22
play [plei] v. : spielen 27, 75, 78, 85, 86
player ['pleiəʳ] n. : Spieler, in 86
playground ['pleigraund] n. : Hof n. m. 27
playroom ['pleiru:m] n. : Spielzimmer n. nt. 75
playtime ['pleitaim] n. : Pause n. f. 27
pocket money ['pɔkit'mʌni] : Taschengeld n. nt. 28
podium pl. **-dia** ['poudiəm, -diə] n. : Podium n. nt. 84
policeman pl. **-men** [p(ə)'li:smæn, -men] n. m. : Polizist 18

police [pə'li:s] n. : Polizei n. f. 65
polite [pə'lait] adj. : höflich 38
pond [pɔnd] n. : Teich n. m. 68
ponytail ['pouniteil] n. : Pferdeschwanz n. m. 37
poor [puəʳ] adj. : arm 38, 77
portrait ['pɔ:treit] n. : Porträt n. nt. 77
postman pl. **-men** ['poustmæn, -men] n. m. : Briefträger 18
post office [poust'ɔfis] n. : Post n. f. 18
potato [p(ə)'teitou] n. : Kartoffel n. f. 52
practical ['præktik(ə)l] adj. : praktisch 55
present ['prezənt] n. : Geschenk n. nt. 90, 92
price [prais] n. : Preis n. m. 9
projector [prə'dʒektəʳ] n. : Projektor n. m. 80
puddle ['pʌdl] n. : Pfütze n. f. 67
pullover ['pulouvəʳ] n. : Pullover n. m. 41
pumpkin ['pʌmpkin] n. : Kürbis n. m. 52
pupil ['pju:p(i)l] n. : Schüler, in 26
purple ['pə:pl] adj. : violett 29
purse [pə:s] n. : Geldbeutel n. m. 21
pushchair [pʌstʃɛəʳ] n. : Kinderwagen n. m. 81
put* [put] v. : legen 27
puzzle ['pʌzl] n. : Puzzle n. nt. 75
pyjamas [pə'dʒɑ:məs] n. pl. : Schlafanzug n. m. 13

Q

question ['kwestʃ(ə)n] n. : Frage n. f. 27
quickly ['kwikli] adv. : schnell 69

R

rabbit ['ræbit] n. : Kaninchen n. nt. 62
race [reis] n. : Lauf n. m. 84
radish ['rædiʃ] n. : Radieschen n. nt. 52
rain [rein] n. : Regen n. m. 52, 67
rain [rein] v. : regnen 52
raincoat ['reinkout] n. : Regenmantel n. m. 40, 67
raise [reiz] n. : Erhöhung n. f. 28
rake [reik] n. : Rechen n. m. 8
read* ['ri:d] v. : lesen* 11
real ['riəl] adj. : echt 57, 64
really ['riəli] adv. : wirklich 55, 77
record [ri'kɔ:d] n. : Platte n. f. 37
rectangle ['rektæŋgl] n. : Rechteck n. nt. 30
red [red] adj. : rot 29
red-haired ['red'hɛəd] adj. : rothaarig 37
rent [rent] v. : mieten 9; vermieten 9, 93
rice [rais] n. : Reis n. m. 56
rich [ritʃ] adj. : reich 38
ride* a horse [raidə'hɔ:s] : reiten* 68
rider ['raidəʳ] n. : Kunstreiter, in 93
ring [riŋ] n. : Ring n. m. 43; Manege n. f. 93
ring* [riŋ] v. : klingeln 12; schlagen* 31
ripe [raip] adj. : reif 53
river ['rivəʳ] n. : Fluß n. m. 64
road sign [roudsain] : Schild n. nt. 23
roll [roul] v. : rollen 43
roller skate ['rouləʳskeit] : Rollschuh n. m. 85
roof [ru:f] n. : Dach n. nt. 9, 68
rose [rouz] n. : Rose n. f. 63
round [raund] adj. : rund 30
rubber ['rʌbəʳ] n. : Radiergummi n. m. 77
rubber ring ['rʌbəʳriŋ] : Schwimmring n. m. 73
ruby ['ru:bi] n. : Rubin n. m. 43
rucksack ['rʌksæk] n. : Rucksack n. m. 74
rug [rʌg] n. : Teppich n. m. 12
ruler ['ru:ləʳ] n. : Lineal n. m. 77
run* [rʌn] v. : laufen* 27, 69, 84

S

sail [seil] n. : Segel n. nt. 65
sale [seil] n. : Schlußverkauf n. m. 31
salesperson [seilz'pə:s(ə)n] n. : Verkäufer, in 21
salt [sɔlt] n. : Salz n. nt. 54
sand [sænd] n. : Sand n. m. 73
sandal ['sænd(ə)l] n. : Sandale n. f. 47
sand castle [sændkɑ:s(ə)l] : Sandburg n. f. 73
sandwich ['sændwitʃ] n. : Sandwich n. nt. 91
satchel ['sætʃ(ə)l] n. : Schulranzen n. m. 28
saucepan ['sɔ:spən] n. : Kochtopf n. m. 14
saxophone ['sæksəfoun] n. : Saxophon n. nt. 79
say* [sei] v. : sagen* 42
school [sku:l] n. : Schule n. f. 25, 26, 27, 30
schoolteacher ['sku:lti:tʃəʳ] n. : Lehrer, in 26
scream [skri:m] v. : schreien* 80
screen [skri:n] n. : Leinwand n. f. 80
sea [si:] n. : Meer n. nt. 65
seagull ['si:gʌl] n. : Möwe n. f. 66
seat [si:t] n. : Sessel n. m. 80
second ['sekənd] n. : Sekunde n. f. 31
second ['sekənd] adj. : zweite(r, s) 93
see* [si:] v. : sehen* 34, 46, 53, 56, 67, 76, 80
see you soon! [si:jusu:n] interj. : bis bald! 8, 22
sell* [sel] v. : verkaufen 9, 21
shampoo [ʃæm'pu:] n. : Shampoo n. nt. 15
shape [ʃeip] n. : Form n. f. 30
sheet [ʃi:t] n. : Laken n. nt. 12
shelf pl. **shelves** [ʃelf, ʃelvz] n. : Regal n. nt. 14
shell [ʃel] n. : Muschel n. f. 73
shine* [ʃain] v. : scheinen* 73; leuchten 66
ship [ʃip] n. : Schiff n. nt. 65
shirt [ʃə:t] n. : Hemd n. nt. 41
shoe [ʃu:] n. : Schuh n. m. 42, 67
shoelace ['ʃu:leis] n. : Schnürsenkel n. m. 42
shop [ʃɔp] n. : Geschäft n. nt. 20; Laden n. m. 20
shop [ʃɔp] v. : einkaufen 20
short [ʃɔ:t] adj. : kurz 37, 40
shorts [ʃɔ:ts] n. pl. : Shorts n. pl. 85
shoulder ['ʃouldəʳ] n. : Schulter n. f. 46
shovel ['ʃʌv(ə)l] n. : Schaufel n. f. 8
show* [ʃou] v. : zeigen 31, 72
show* the way [ʃouðə'wei] : den Weg zeigen 18
shutter ['ʃʌtəʳ] n. : Fensterladen n. m. 9
sick [sik] adj. : krank 49
sing* [siŋ] : singen* 79
singer ['siŋəʳ] n. : Sänger, in 79
sink [siŋk] n. : Spüle n. f. 14
sink* [siŋk] v. : sinken* 64
be* **sitting down** [bi:sitiŋdaun] : sitzen* 11
sitting-room [sitiŋru:m] n. : Wohnzimmer n. nt. 11, 69
skate board ['skeitbɔ:d] : Skateboard n. nt. 85
ski [ski] n. : Schi n. m. 87
ski [ski] v. : Schi laufen 87
ski hat [skihæt] : Schimütze 87
skiing [skiiŋ] n. : Schifahren n. nt. 87
skirt [skə:t] n. : Rock n. m. 40
sky [skai] n. : Himmel n. m. 66
sleep* [sli:p] v. : schlafen* 13, 74
sleeping bag ['sli:piŋbæg] : Schlafsack n. m. 74
sleepwalker ['sli:pwɔ:kəʳ] n. : Schlafwandler n. m. 57
sleigh [slait] n. : Schlitten n. m. 87
slide [slaid] n. : Rutschbahn n. f. 81; Haarspange n. f. 37
slide* [slaid] v. : rutschen 81
slipper ['slipəʳ] n. : Hausschuh n. m. 41
slope [sloup] n. : Piste n. f. 87
small [smɔ:l] adj. : klein 36
smart [smɑ:t] adj. : elegant 39
smile [smail] v. : lächeln 91
smock [smɔk] n. : Kittel n. m. 77
smoke [smouk] n. : Rauch n. m. 74
snake [sneik] n. : Schlange n. f. 69
snow [snou] n. : Schnee n. m. 87
snow [snou] v. : schneien 87
snowball ['snoubɔ:l] n. : Schneeball n. m. 87
snowman pl. **-men** [snoumæn, -men] n. m. : Schneemann 87

soap [soup] n. : Seife n. f. **15**
sock [sɔk] n. : Socke n. f. **41**
solution [sə'luːʃ(ə)n] n. : Lösung n. f. **55**
son [sʌn] n. m. : Sohn **34**
soon [suːn] adv. : bald **12**
be*sorry [biː'sɔri] : leid tun* **38**
soup [suːp] n. : Suppe n. f. **57**
soup tureen [suːptjuə'riːn] : Suppenschüssel n. f. **57**
spectator [spek'teitər] n. : Zuschauer, in **93**
sponge [spʌn(d)ʒ] n. : Schwamm n. m. **14**
spoon [spuːn] n. : Löffel n. m. **54**
sport [spɔːt] n. : Sport n. m. **83**
sportsgear [spɔːtsgiər] n. : Ausrüstung n. f. **85**
spring ['spriŋ] n. : Frühling n. m. **8**
square ['skwɛər] n. : Quadrat n. nt. **30**
squirrel ['skwir(ə)l] n. : Eichhörnchen n. nt. **60**
stadium ['steidiəm] n. : Sportplatz n. m. **84**
stag [stæg] n. : Hirsch n. m. **76**
stage [steidʒ] n. : Bühne n. f. **78**
stain [stein] n. : Fleck n. m. **77**
stairs ['stəz] n. pl. : Treppe n. f. **10**
stamp [stæmp] n. : Briefmarke n. f. **21**
stand* [stænd] v. : aushalten* **42**
be*standing up [biːstændiŋʌp] : stehen* **47**
star [staːʳ] n. : Stern n. m. **66**
starch [staːtʃ] n. : Stärke n. f. **87**
starving ['staːviŋ] adj. : hungrig **77**
station ['steiʃ(ə)n] n. : Bahnhof n. m. **22**
stem [stem] n. : Stengel n. m. **63**
step [step] n. : Stufe n. f. **10**
stereo ['steriou] n. : Stereoanlage n. f. **11**
stomach ['stʌmək] n. : Bauch n. m. **46**
stool [stuːl] n. : Hocker n. m. **14**
storm [stɔːm] n. : Sturm n. m. **67**
straight [streit] adj. : glatt **37**
strange [strein(d)ʒ] adj. : seltsam **42**
strawberry ['strɔːb(ə)ri] n. : Erdbeere n. f. **53**
street [striːt] n. : Straße n. f. **18, 93**
stripe [straip] n. : Streifen n. m. **29**
strong [strɔŋ] adj. : stark **36, 85**
stuff [stʌf] v. : füllen **20**
stuffing ['stʌfiŋ] n. : Füllung n. f. **20**
sturdy ['stəːdi] adj. : stabil **64**
subtraction [səb'trækʃ(ə)n] n. : Subtrahieren n. nt. **28**
sugar ['ʃugər] n. : Zucker n. m. **21, 55**
sugar dispenser ['ʃugərdis'pensər] : Zuckerdose n. f. **55**
suit [s(j)uːt] n. : Anzug **39, 41**
suitcase ['s(j)uːtkeis] n. : Koffer n. m. **22**
summer ['sʌmər] n. : Sommer n. m. **73**
sun [sʌn] n. : Sonne n. f. **62, 73**
sunglasses ['sʌnglaːsiz] n. pl. : Sonnenbrille n. f. **73**
sun-tanned ['sʌntænd] adj. : braun **73**
supermarket [s(j)uː'pəmaːkit] n. : Supermarkt n. m. **20**
sure ['ʃuər] adj. : sicher **20**
surprise [sə'praiz] n. : Überraschung n. f. **14, 38**
sweet [swiːt] n. : Bonbon n. m. **28, 92**
sweet pepper [swiːt'pepər] : Paprika n. m. **52**
swim* [swim] v. : schwimmen* **65, 68**
swing [swiŋ] n. : Schaukel n. f. **81**
synthesizer ['sinθəsaizər] n. : Synthesizer n. m. **79**
syringe ['sirindʒ, si'rindʒ] n. : Spritze n. f. **49**

T

table ['teibl] n. : Tisch n. m. **54**
tablecloth ['teiblklɔθ] n. : Tischdecke n. f. **56**
table tennis ['teibl'tenis] : Tischtennis n. nt. **86**
take*off ['teikɔf] v. : starten **72**
tall [tɔːl] adj. : groß **36**
tamer ['teimər] n. : Dompteur n. m. **93**
tap [tæp] n. : Wasserhahn n. m. **15**

tart [taːt] n. : Obsttorte n. f. **56**
taxi ['tæksi] n. : Taxi n. nt. **23**
tea [tiː] n. : Tee n. m. **55**
teacher ['tiːtʃər] n. : Lehrer, in **27**
teapot ['tiːpɔt] n. : Teekanne n. f. **55**
teddy bear ['tedibɛər] : Teddybär n. m. **75**
tee-shirt ['tiːʃəːt] n. : T-Shirt n. nt. **41**
telephone ['telifoun] n. : Telefon n. nt. **11**
make*a **telephone call** [meikə'telifounkɔːl] : telefonieren **19**
telephone kiosk [founbɔks] : Telefonzelle n. f. **19**
television [teli'viʒ(ə)n] n. : Fernseher n. m. **11**
tell* [tel] v. : sagen **52**
tennis shoe ['tenisʃuː] : Sportschuh n. m. **42**
tent [tent] n. : Zelt n. nt. **74**
thanks! [θæŋks] interj. : danke! **28, 36**
thin [θin] adj. : dünn **36**
think* [θiŋk] v. : denken* **87**; glauben* **35, 43**
be*thirsty [biː'θəːsti] : durstig sein* **54**; Durst haben* **81**
throw* [θrou] v. : werfen* **87**
thunder ['θʌndər] n. : Donner n. m. **67**
ticket collector ['tikitkə'lektər] : Schaffner, in **22**
tie [tai] n. : Krawatte n. f. **39**
tights [taits] n. pl. : Strumpfhose n. f. **39**
time [taim] n. : Zeit n. f. **14**; Uhrzeit n. f. **31**
tired ['taid] adj. : müde **13**
today [tə'dei] adv. : heute **27, 60, 72**
toe [tou] n. : Zehe n. f. **47**
tomato [tə'maːtou] n. : Tomate n. f. **91**
tomorrow [tə'mɔrou] adv. : morgen **31, 52**
tongue [tʌŋ] n. : Zunge n. f. **48**
tonight [tə'nait] adv. : heute abend **39**
too [tuː] adv. : zu **40, 42, 62, 85**; auch **75**
tooth pl. **teeth** [tuːθ, tiːθ] n. : Zahn n. m. **15, 48**
toothbrush ['tuːθbrʌʃ] n. : Zahnbürste n. f. **15**
toothpaste ['tuːθpeist] n. : Zahnpasta n. f. **15**
total ['tout(ə)l] n. : Summe n. f. **28**
towel ['tauəl] n. : Handtuch n. nt. **15**
town [taun] n. : Stadt n. f. **17, 29**
toys [tɔiz] n. pl. : Spielsache n. f. **75**
track [træk] n. : Spur n. f. **30**; Rennbahn n. f. **84**; Weg n. m. **61**; Gleis n. nt. **22**
tracksuit ['træks(j)uːt] n. : Trainingsanzug n. m. **85**
traffic ['træfik] n. : Verkehr n. m. **19**
traffic jam ['træfikdʒæm] : Stau n. m. **18, 19**
(traffic) light [('træfik)lait] n. : Ampel n. f. **18**
train [trein] n. : Zug n. m. **22**
transport ['trænspɔːt] n. : Verkehrsmittel n. nt. **23**
tree [triː] n. : Baum n. m. **8, 60, 90**
triangle ['traiæŋgl] n. : Dreieck n. nt. **30**
trousers ['trauzəz] n. pl. : Hose n. f. **40**
trumpet ['trʌmpit] n. : Trompete n. f. **78**
trunk [trʌŋk] n. : Stamm n. m. **60**
try* [trai] v. : versuchen* **65**
tube of paint [tjuːbɔvpeint] : Farbtube n. f. **77**
tulip ['tjuːlip] n. : Tulpe n. f. **63**
turkey ['təːki] n. : Pute n. f. **90**
tyre ['taiər] n. : Reifen n. m. **19**

U

ugly ['ʌgli] adj. : häßlich **36**
umbrella [ʌm'brelə] n. : Regenschirm n. m. **67**
umpire ['ʌmpaiər] n. : Schiedsrichter n. m. **86**
uncle ['ʌŋkl] n. : Onkel n. m. **14, 34**
understand* [ʌndə'stænd] v. : verstehen* **30**

V

valley ['væli] n. : Tal n. nt. **61**
vase [vaːz] n. : Vase n. f. **11**

vegetables ['vedʒ(i)təbls] n. pl. : Gemüse n. nt. **52**
very ['veri] adv. : sehr **39, 62**
vest [vest] n. : Trikot n. m. **85**
viewer ['vjuər] n. : Zuschauer, in **80**
violin [vaiə'lin] n. : Geige n. f. **78**

W

wait (for) [weit(fɔːʳ)] v. : warten **23, 60, 62, 69, 92**
wake*up ['weikʌp] v. : wach werden* **12**
walkie-talkie [wɔːki'tɔki] n. : Walkie-talkie n. nt. **61**
wall [wɔːl] n. : Mauer n. f. **9**
wallet ['wɔlit] n. : Brieftasche n. f. **21**
wallpaper ['wɔːlpeipər] n. : Tapete n. f. **69**
want [wɔnt] v. : wollen* **20, 29, 53**
wardrobe ['wɔːdroub] n. : Kleiderschrank n. m. **41**; Schrank n. m. **12**
warm oneself [wɔːmwʌn'self] v. : sich wärmen **74**
wash oneself [wɔʃwʌn'self] v. : sich waschen* **15**
watch [wɔtʃ] n. : Uhr n. f. **31, 48**
watch (over) [wɔtʃ('ouvər)] v. : beaufsichtigen **27**
watch television [wɔtʃteli'viʒ(ə)n] : fernsehen **11**
water ['wɔːtər] n. : Wasser n. nt. **57**
water ['wɔːtər] v. : gießen* **8**
watering can ['wɔːtəriŋkæn] : Gießkanne n. f. **8**
water-ski* ['wɔːtəʳskiː] v. : Wasserschi fahren* **65**
wear* [wɛəʳ] v. : tragen* **39, 46**
weather ['weðər] n. : Wetter n. nt. **67**
weathercock ['weðəkɔk] n. : Wetterhahn n. m. **68**
week [wiːk] n. : Woche n. f. **28**
weigh [wei] v. : wiegen* **20**
weights [weits] n. pl. : Hanteln n. f. pl. **85**
well [wel] adv. : gut **34, 77, 86**
wet [wet] adj. : naß **67**
white [(h)wait] adj. : weiß **29**
wife pl. **wives** [waif, waivz] n. f. : Frau **34**
wild [waild] adj. : wild **69**
wilted ['wiltid] adj. : verblüht **63**
win* [win] v. : gewinnen* **84, 86**
wind [wind] n. : Wind n. m. **65**
window ['windou] n. : Fenster n. nt. **9**
winner ['winər] n. : Sieger n. m. **84**
winter ['wintər] n. : Winter n. m. **87**
woman pl. **-men** ['wumən, -min] n. f. : Frau **35, 72**; Dame **22**
wood [wud] n. : Holz n. nt. **74**
work [wəːk] n. : Arbeit n. f. **52**
work hard [wəːkhaːd] : fleißig sein* **26**
worried ['wʌrid] adj. : beunruhigt **49**
write* [rait] v. : schreiben* **26**

Y

yawn [jɔːn] v. : gähnen **13**
yellow ['jelou] adj. : gelb **29**
yogurt ['jɔgət] n. : Yoghurt n. m. **56**
young [jʌŋ] adj. : jung **35**

Z

zebra ['ziːbrə] n. : Zebra n. nt. **69, 76**
zebra crossing ['ziːbrəkrɔsiŋ] : Zebrastreifen n. m. **23**
zoo [zuː] n. : Zoo n. m. **76**

Printed in Spain
by Graficromo, S. A. Córdoba